AF410294

ONE

INTRODUCTION

The dawn of the 21st century has witnessed a profound transformation in the way we interact with and shape our environment. This transformation is driven by the burgeoning field of Cyber-Physical Systems (CPS), a paradigm that seamlessly integrates computational algorithms with physical processes. No longer confined to the realm of theoretical constructs, CPS are rapidly permeating every facet of modern life, from the intricate workings of smart grids that power our cities to the autonomous vehicles that promise to revolutionize transportation, and the sophisticated medical devices that are extending the boundaries of healthcare. This book, "Intelligent Cyber-Physical Systems: A Practical Guide to Smart Automation and Security," aims to illuminate the intricate pathways of this transformative domain, providing a comprehensive and practical roadmap for navigating the complexities of CPS design, implementation, and security.

At its core, a CPS represents a synergistic fusion of computation, communication, and control, allowing for the real-time monitoring and manipulation of physical systems through intelligent software. This integration enables the creation of systems that are not only responsive and efficient but also adaptable and intelligent. The ability to collect, process, and act upon vast amounts of data from the physical world empowers CPS to optimize processes, predict failures, and even self-heal in the face of unforeseen challenges.

However, the very characteristics that make CPS so powerful also introduce a unique set of challenges. The tight coupling between the digital and physical realms creates a complex ecosystem where failures in one domain can cascade into the other, potentially leading to catastrophic consequences. Moreover, the increasing reliance on interconnected networks and cloud-based services exposes CPS to a myriad of cybersecurity threats, demanding robust security measures to safeguard critical infrastructure and sensitive data.

This book is structured to guide the reader through the multifaceted landscape of CPS, starting with a solid foundation in the fundamental principles and architectures that underpin these systems. We will explore the essential components, including sensors, actuators, embedded systems, and communication networks, and delve into the techniques for data acquisition, processing, and analysis. Building upon this foundation, we will then delve into the realm of intelligent automation, examining how machine learning and artificial intelligence can be leveraged to enhance the capabilities of CPS. From predictive maintenance and adaptive control to optimization and decision-making, we will explore practical applications of AI that are transforming industries and improving lives.

However, the pursuit of intelligent automation cannot come at the expense of security. As CPS become increasingly interconnected and sophisticated, they also become more vulnerable to cyberattacks. We will dedicate significant attention to the critical aspects of cybersecurity, exploring the various threats and vulnerabilities that plague CPS, and providing practical guidance on implementing robust security mechanisms and protocols. From authentication and access control to encryption and intrusion detection, we will equip readers with the knowledge and tools necessary to build resilient and secure CPS.

Furthermore, we recognize that the true potential of CPS can only be realized through practical implementation. Therefore, this book goes beyond theoretical concepts and provides concrete

INTELLIGENT CYBER PHYSICAL SYSTEM: A PRACTICAL GUIDE TO SMART AUTOMATION AND SECURITY

M.MARANCO

P.SAVARIDASSAN

M.SIVAKUMAR

N.KRISHNARAJ

Copyright © M.Maranco,P.Savaridassan, M.Sivakumar, N.Krishnaraj
All Rights Reserved.

This book has been self-published with all reasonable efforts taken to make the material error-free by the author. No part of this book shall be used, reproduced in any manner whatsoever without written permission from the author, except in the case of brief quotations embodied in critical articles and reviews.

The Author of this book is solely responsible and liable for its content including but not limited to the views, representations, descriptions, statements, information, opinions and references ["Content"]. The Content of this book shall not constitute or be construed or deemed to reflect the opinion or expression of the Publisher or Editor. Neither the Publisher nor Editor endorse or approve the Content of this book or guarantee the reliability, accuracy or completeness of the Content published herein and do not make any representations or warranties of any kind, express or implied, including but not limited to the implied warranties of merchantability, fitness for a particular purpose. The Publisher and Editor shall not be liable whatsoever for any errors, omissions, whether such errors or omissions result from negligence, accident, or any other cause or claims for loss or damages of any kind, including without limitation, indirect or consequential loss or damage arising out of use, inability to use, or about the reliability, accuracy or sufficiency of the information contained in this book.

Made with ❤ on the Notion Press Platform
www.notionpress.com

Contents

examples, case studies, and practical guidance on developing and deploying CPS in real-world scenarios. We will explore the latest development tools and platforms, and examine successful implementations in diverse domains such as smart grids, autonomous vehicles, and industrial automation. By bridging the gap between theory and practice, we aim to empower readers to not only understand the principles of CPS but also to apply them effectively in their own projects and research.

As we venture further into the age of interconnected intelligence, the importance of CPS will only continue to grow. This book is intended to serve as a comprehensive and practical guide for professionals, researchers, and enthusiasts who are eager to explore the transformative potential of CPS and contribute to the development of a smarter, more secure, and more sustainable future. By providing a clear and accessible roadmap through the complexities of CPS, we hope to inspire and empower the next generation of innovators to shape the world with intelligent and secure cyber-physical systems.

TWO

FOUNDATIONS OF CYBER PHYSICAL SYSTEMS (CPS)

The bedrock upon which the edifice of intelligent, interconnected systems rests is the fundamental understanding of Cyber-Physical Systems (CPS). Before we can delve into the intricate applications of AI-driven automation or the critical safeguarding of these systems against cyber threats, we must first establish a firm grasp of the core principles that define and govern CPS. This section, "Foundations of Cyber-Physical Systems (CPS)," is dedicated to laying that groundwork, providing a comprehensive exploration of the essential components, architectures, and data processing techniques that form the very essence of this transformative field. We embark on a journey that transcends the mere definition of CPS, venturing into the historical evolution, the diverse application domains, and the technological underpinnings that enable their functionality.

The concept of integrating computational elements with physical processes is not entirely new. Embedded systems, for instance, have long been used to control and monitor physical devices. However, the emergence of CPS marks a significant paradigm shift. It represents a move beyond isolated, task-specific embedded systems towards a more holistic and interconnected approach, where physical systems are seamlessly integrated with the digital world through sophisticated communication networks and intelligent software. This integration enables the creation of systems that are not only responsive to their environment but also capable of adapting and evolving over time. The ability to collect and analyze vast amounts of real-time data from the physical world empowers CPS to optimize performance, predict failures, and even self-regulate, leading to unprecedented levels of efficiency and reliability.

Understanding the architecture of a CPS is crucial to comprehending its functionality. We will dissect the essential components, starting with the sensors and actuators that serve as the interface between the physical and digital realms. Sensors provide the means to gather data from the environment, while actuators enable the system to exert control over physical processes. We will then explore the communication networks that facilitate the exchange of data between these components, including both wired and wireless technologies. Furthermore, we will delve into the realm of embedded systems and microcontrollers, the computational engines that process data and execute control algorithms. The rise of cloud computing and edge computing has further expanded the capabilities of CPS, enabling distributed intelligence and scalable data processing. We will examine how these technologies are integrated into CPS architectures, and explore the various architectural models, including layered, distributed, and hybrid approaches.

Beyond the hardware and communication infrastructure, the ability to effectively acquire, process, and analyze data is paramount to the success of a CPS. We will explore the techniques for sensor data acquisition, including sampling, quantization, and noise reduction. Signal processing and filtering methods will be discussed, enabling the extraction of meaningful features from raw sensor data. The importance of data storage and management will be highlighted, covering topics such as databases, data warehousing, and big data solutions. Finally, we will examine data analytics and visualization techniques, empowering users to extract insights from the vast amounts of data generated by CPS.

The foundation laid in this section is not merely theoretical. It is the necessary prerequisite for understanding the more advanced topics that follow. Without a solid grasp of the fundamental principles of CPS, it is impossible to fully appreciate the potential of intelligent automation or the importance of cybersecurity. By exploring the core components, architectures, and data processing techniques that underpin CPS, we are building a bridge between the physical and digital worlds, paving the way for the development of innovative and transformative technologies. This journey into the foundations of CPS will provide the reader with a comprehensive understanding of the building blocks that are shaping the future of our interconnected world, setting the stage for the practical exploration of smart automation and security that will follow. This initial exploration will ensure that the reader has the core knowledge needed to fully understand the complexities and nuances of the more advanced implementations covered in the later sections of this book.

INTRODUCTION TO CYBER-PHYSICAL SYSTEMS

To truly grasp the significance of Cyber-Physical Systems (CPS), it's essential to move beyond a simple definition and delve into the nuances of their operation and impact.

The concept of "bridging the physical and digital worlds" is fundamental to understanding the transformative power of modern technology, particularly in the context of Cyber-Physical Systems (CPS) and the Internet of Things (IoT). Here's a breakdown of what that entails:

Core Idea:

Essentially, it's about creating a seamless interaction between our tangible, real-world environment and the intangible realm of digital information and processes.

This involves:

- Sensing the Physical: Gathering data from the physical world using sensors (e.g., temperature, pressure, motion).
- Digitizing the Data: Converting that physical data into a digital format that computers can understand.
- Processing and Analysis: Using software and algorithms to analyze the digital data and extract meaningful insights.
- Actuating in the Physical: Using actuators (e.g., motors, valves) to translate digital commands back into physical actions, influencing the real world.
- Networking: Connecting all those components together so that they can communicate and exchange information.

Key Technologies and Examples:

Internet of Things (IoT):

IoT devices are embedded with sensors and actuators, enabling them to collect and exchange data over the internet.

Examples: Smart home devices, industrial sensors, wearable fitness trackers.

Cyber-Physical Systems (CPS):

CPS involve a deeper integration of computation and physical processes, often with real-time feedback loops.

Examples: Autonomous vehicles, smart grids, advanced manufacturing systems.

Digital Twins:

Digital twins are virtual replicas of physical objects or systems, allowing for simulation, analysis, and optimization. They provide a way to understand and predict the behavior of physical systems in a digital environment.

Augmented Reality (AR):

AR overlays digital information onto the real world, enhancing our perception of our surroundings.

Examples: AR apps that provide directions, virtual try-on tools for online shopping.

Impact and Significance:

- Optimizing processes in industries like manufacturing, transportation, and energy.
- Monitoring critical infrastructure, detecting potential hazards, and preventing accidents.
- Creating more personalized and interactive experiences in areas like retail, entertainment, and healthcare.
- Providing real-time insights that enable better decision-making in various domains.

In essence, bridging the physical and digital worlds is about creating a more intelligent and responsive environment, where technology seamlessly integrates with our daily lives.

Key Characteristics: Integration, Real-Time, and Feedback Loops

When discussing Cyber-Physical Systems (CPS), three key characteristics consistently emerge: integration, real-time operation, and feedback loops. These elements are fundamental to understanding how CPS function and why they are so impactful. Here's a deeper look:

1. Integration:

Cyber and Physical Fusion:

This refers to the seamless merging of computational (cyber) elements with physical processes. It's not just about connecting devices; it's about creating a unified system where the digital and physical components are deeply intertwined.

This integration allows for a bidirectional flow of information and control. The physical world provides data to the cyber world, and the cyber world uses that data to influence the physical world.

Interconnectedness:

CPS often involve networks of interconnected devices, sensors, and actuators. This interconnectedness enables them to monitor and control large-scale systems. This also means that the system as a whole is more than the sum of its parts. Individual components work together to achieve a common goal.

2. Real-Time Operation:

Timely Responses:

Many CPS operate in dynamic environments where timely responses are critical. They must be able to process data and react to events in real-time. This requires high-performance computing, low-latency communication, and efficient algorithms.

Time-Critical Applications:

Real-time operation is particularly important in safety-critical applications, such as autonomous vehicles and industrial control systems. In these applications, even small delays can have significant consequences.

3. Feedback Loops:

Closed-Loop Control:

Feedback loops are essential for regulating and optimizing physical processes. Sensors provide data on the current state of the system, and this data is used to adjust the actuators. This closed-loop control allows CPS to adapt to changing conditions and maintain desired performance levels.

Continuous Monitoring and Adjustment:

Feedback loops enable continuous monitoring and adjustment of physical processes. This allows CPS to:

- Maintain stability.
- Optimize performance.
- Detect and correct errors.

Example:

Think of a thermostat. It senses the room's temperature, compares it to the desired temperature, and then turns the heating or cooling system on or off accordingly. This is a simple example of a feedback loop.

Evolution of CPS

1. Embedded Systems:

Focus:

These systems are designed for specific, often single-purpose tasks within a larger system. They emphasize reliability and efficiency in a constrained environment. Early examples were often electromechanical, with limited computational capabilities.

Examples:

Anti-lock braking systems (ABS) in cars: A dedicated computer monitors wheel speed and prevents lockups.

Microwave oven controllers: A simple embedded system manages cooking time and power levels.

Early pacemakers: Implanted devices with basic electronic control of heart rhythm.

Limitations:

- Isolated operation: They typically don't communicate with other systems.
- Limited adaptability: They are designed for fixed tasks.
- Basic processing: Early embedded systems had limited computational power.

2. Networked Embedded Systems:

The introduction of networking enabled embedded systems to share data and coordinate actions. This led to the development of distributed control systems, where multiple embedded systems work together. Industrial applications saw significant advancements.

Examples:

SCADA (Supervisory Control and Data Acquisition) systems: Used in industrial settings to monitor and control processes like power generation and water treatment.

Building automation systems: Networks of sensors and controllers that manage HVAC, lighting, and security.

Early automotive networks (e.g., CAN bus): Enabling communication between different electronic control units (ECUs) in a vehicle.

Advancements:

- Increased system-level control: Enables optimization of larger processes.
- Remote monitoring and management: Allows for centralized control of distributed systems.
- Data collection and analysis: Enables better understanding of system performance.

3. Cyber-Physical Systems: The Integration Era

CPS represent a more profound integration of computation and physical processes, with real-time feedback loops. They emphasize adaptability, autonomy, and resilience. AI and machine learning play an increasingly important role.

Examples:

Autonomous vehicles: Complex CPS that use sensors, AI, and control algorithms to navigate and drive.

Smart grids: Intelligent power distribution systems that optimize energy flow and integrate renewable energy sources.

Advanced robotics: Robots that can adapt to changing environments and perform complex tasks.

Precision agriculture: Systems that use sensors and data analysis to optimize crop yields and resource utilization.

Key Features:

- Real-time feedback: Enables continuous monitoring and control.
- Adaptive control: Allows systems to adjust to changing conditions.
- Increased autonomy: Enables systems to make decisions and take actions without human intervention.

4. Smart Environments: The Ubiquitous CPS

The proliferation of IoT devices and cloud computing has led to the development of smart environments, where CPS are integrated into our daily lives. These environments are characterized by ubiquitous sensing, connectivity, and intelligence. They are designed to improve quality of life, sustainability, and efficiency.

Examples:

Smart homes: Connected devices that automate tasks and improve comfort and security.

Smart cities: Urban environments that use CPS to manage traffic, energy, and public services.

Smart factories (Industry 4.0): Highly automated and interconnected manufacturing facilities.

Smart healthcare: Wearable devices, remote patient monitoring, and AI-powered diagnostics.

Enablers:

- IoT platforms: Enable connectivity and data management.
- Cloud computing: Provides scalable computing and storage resources.
- Edge computing: Enables distributed intelligence and real-time processing.
- AI and machine learning: Enable data analysis, decision-making, and automation.

This extended explanation provides a more detailed understanding of the evolution of CPS, highlighting the key advancements and trends that have shaped this transformative field.

Applications Across Industries

Cyber-Physical Systems (CPS) are revolutionizing numerous industries by seamlessly integrating computation, networking, and physical processes. This integration allows for real-time monitoring, control, and optimization, leading to significant improvements in efficiency, safety, and productivity. Here's a look at how CPS are transforming key sectors:

1. Healthcare:

Remote Patient Monitoring:

Wearable sensors and IoT devices collect vital health data, enabling remote monitoring of patients with chronic conditions.

This allows for early detection of health issues and timely intervention.

Smart Medical Devices:

CPS are used in advanced medical devices, such as insulin pumps and pacemakers, to provide precise and personalized treatments. Robotic surgery systems enhance surgical precision and minimize invasiveness.

Hospital Automation: CPS optimize hospital operations by automating tasks like medication dispensing, patient tracking, and resource management.

2. Manufacturing:

Industry 4.0: CPS are a core component of Industry 4.0, enabling smart factories with interconnected machines and systems. This leads to increased automation, flexibility, and efficiency.

Predictive Maintenance: Sensors monitor equipment conditions, and data analytics predict when maintenance is needed, reducing downtime and costs.

Quality Control: Automated inspection systems use sensors and AI to detect defects in products, ensuring high quality.

Supply Chain Optimization: CPS helps to track inventory in real time, and helps to automate the reordering process.

3. Transportation:

Autonomous Vehicles: CPS are the foundation of self-driving cars, using sensors, AI, and control algorithms to navigate and drive.

Smart Traffic Management: CPS optimize traffic flow by using sensors and data analytics to adjust traffic signals and manage congestion.

Connected Vehicles: Vehicle-to-vehicle (V2V) and vehicle-to-infrastructure (V2I) communication enhance safety and efficiency.

Logistics and Supply Chain: CPS helps to track the location of goods in real time, and optimizes delivery routes.

4. Smart Grids:

Energy Efficiency: CPS optimize energy distribution by monitoring and controlling power flow in real-time.

Renewable Energy Integration: CPS enable the integration of renewable energy sources, such as solar and wind power, into the grid.

Grid Resilience: CPS enhance grid resilience by detecting and responding to faults and outages.

5. Agriculture:

Precision Agriculture: Sensors and data analytics optimize crop yields by monitoring soil conditions, weather patterns, and plant health.

Automated Farming: Robots and drones automate tasks like planting, watering, and harvesting.

These are just a few examples of how CPS are transforming industries. As technology continues to advance, we can expect to see even more innovative applications of CPS in the future.

CORE COMPONENTS AND ARCHITECTURE

Understanding the core components and architecture of Cyber-Physical Systems (CPS) is akin to dissecting the anatomy of a complex organism. It's the essential first step in comprehending how these systems seamlessly bridge the gap between the digital and physical worlds. This chapter delves into the fundamental building blocks that enable CPS to function, interact, and perform their intended tasks. We will explore the intricate interplay between sensors, actuators, communication networks, embedded systems, and the increasingly vital roles of cloud and edge computing.

The architecture of a CPS is not merely a collection of individual parts; it's a carefully orchestrated system designed to facilitate the flow of information and control. [1] From the initial capture of physical data by sensors to the final actuation that influences the environment, each component plays a crucial role. We will examine how these components are interconnected and how their interactions contribute to the overall functionality and performance of the CPS.

Furthermore, we will explore various architectural models that guide the design and implementation of CPS, ranging from layered and distributed architectures to hybrid approaches that combine the strengths of different paradigms. This exploration will provide a comprehensive understanding of the diverse ways in which CPS can be structured to meet the specific requirements of different applications. By understanding the core components and architectural principles, we can gain valuable insights into the design, implementation, and optimization of these transformative systems, paving the way for the development of more intelligent, efficient, and reliable cyber-physical solutions.

SENSORS AND ACTUATORS:

Sensors and actuators are the vital bridge between the digital core of a Cyber-Physical System (CPS) and the physical world it interacts with. They are, in essence, the "eyes and hands" of the system, enabling it to perceive and manipulate its environment.

Sensors

Function:

Sensors are devices that detect and measure physical quantities or properties, such as temperature, pressure, light, motion, and sound. They convert these physical measurements into electrical signals that can be processed by the digital components of the CPS.

Types:

- **Temperature Sensors:** Thermistors, thermocouples, and resistance temperature detectors (RTDs) measure temperature variations.
- **Pressure Sensors:** Strain gauges and piezoelectric sensors measure pressure changes.
- **Light Sensors:** Photodiodes and phototransistors detect light intensity.
- **Motion Sensors:** Accelerometers, gyroscopes, and magnetometers measure motion and orientation.
- **Proximity Sensors:** Infrared, ultrasonic, and capacitive sensors detect the presence of objects.
- **Chemical Sensors:** Detect the presence and concentration of specific chemicals.

Importance:

- Sensors provide the raw data that the CPS uses to understand its environment.
- The accuracy and reliability of sensors are critical for the overall performance of the CPS.
- Sensor fusion, which is the combining of data from multiple sensors, allows for a more complete and robust understanding of the surrounding environment.

Actuators:

Function:

Actuators are devices that convert electrical signals into physical actions, such as motion, force, or heat. They enable the CPS to manipulate and control its environment.

Types:

- **Motors:** Electric motors are used to generate rotational motion.
- **Linear Actuators:** Solenoids and pneumatic cylinders generate linear motion.
- **Valves:** Control the flow of fluids or gases.
- **Relays:** Electrically controlled switches.
- **Heaters and Coolers:** Control temperature.
- **Speakers:** Convert electrical signals into sound.

Importance:

- Actuators allow the CPS to take action based on the data it receives from sensors and the decisions made by its digital components.
- The precision and responsiveness of actuators are crucial for the effectiveness of the CPS.
- Actuators are what allow the system to have a physical effect on the world around it.

The Interface:

Bidirectional Flow: Sensors and actuators work together to create a bidirectional flow of information and control between the digital and physical worlds. Sensors provide feedback to the digital components, which then use actuators to adjust the physical environment.

Real-Time Interaction: In many CPS, sensors and actuators must operate in real-time to ensure timely responses to events in the physical world.

Critical Role: The quality of the sensor and actuator interface directly impacts the overall performance and reliability of the CPS. The correct sensor and actuator must be chosen for the job at hand.

COMMUNICATION NETWORKS

Communication networks are the lifeblood of Cyber-Physical Systems (CPS), providing the essential pathways for data exchange between sensors, actuators, processing units, and other components. Without robust and reliable communication networks, CPS would be fragmented and unable to function effectively. Here's a deeper look:

Function and Importance:

Data Transmission: Communication networks enable the transmission of data from sensors to processing units, from processing units to actuators, and between different components of the CPS. This data exchange is essential for monitoring, control, and coordination.

Interconnectivity: Networks connect diverse components, allowing them to work together as a cohesive system. This interconnectivity is crucial for complex CPS that involve multiple sensors, actuators, and processing units.

Real-Time Communication: Many CPS require real-time communication to ensure timely responses to events in the physical world. Low-latency and high-bandwidth networks are essential for these applications.

Scalability: Communication networks must be scalable to accommodate the increasing number of devices and data volume in

CPS.

Types of Networks:
Wired Networks:

- **Ethernet:** Widely used for local area networks (LANs) in industrial and commercial settings.
- **CAN (Controller Area Network):** Commonly used in automotive and industrial applications for reliable communication between embedded systems.
- **Fieldbus:** Various industrial communication protocols (e.g., Profibus, Modbus) used for connecting sensors and actuators.

Wireless Networks:

Wi-Fi: Used for wireless connectivity in various applications, including smart homes and industrial settings.

Bluetooth: Used for short-range communication between devices, such as sensors and mobile devices.

Zigbee: Used for low-power, low-data-rate communication in sensor networks and home automation.

Cellular Networks (4G/5G): Used for long-range communication in applications such as autonomous vehicles and smart grids.

LPWAN (Low-Power Wide-Area Networks): (e.g. LoRaWAN, NB-IoT) Used for long-range, low-power communication in IoT applications.

Specialized Networks:

- Time-Sensitive Networking (TSN): Designed for real-time communication in industrial and automotive applications.
- Data Distribution Service (DDS): Used for real-time data distribution in complex CPS.
- MQTT (Message Queuing Telemetry Transport): a light weight messaging protocol used extensively in IOT.

EMBEDDED SYSTEMS AND MICROCONTROLLERS

Embedded systems and microcontrollers are the computational heart of many Cyber-Physical Systems (CPS). They provide the processing power necessary to analyze sensor data, execute control algorithms, and manage communication networks. Here's a deeper dive:

Embedded Systems: Dedicated Computing

An embedded system is a computer system designed for a specific function within a larger mechanical or electrical system. Unlike general-purpose computers, embedded systems are dedicated to a particular task and are often subject to real-time constraints.

Characteristics:

- **Dedicated Function:** Designed for a specific purpose.
- **Real-Time Operation:** Often required to respond to events in a timely manner.
- **Resource Constraints:** Typically have limited memory, processing power, and power consumption.
- **Reliability:** Must operate reliably in harsh environments.

Examples:

- Automotive control systems (e.g., engine control units, airbag controllers).
- Medical devices (e.g., pacemakers, infusion pumps).
- Industrial control systems (e.g., PLCs).
- Consumer electronics (e.g., digital cameras, washing machines).

Microcontrollers:

A microcontroller is a small, integrated circuit that combines a CPU, memory, and peripherals on a single chip. They are the core processing units within many embedded systems.

Key Features:

- **Integrated Peripherals:** Include analog-to-digital converters (ADCs), digital-to-analog converters (DACs), timers, and communication interfaces.
- **Low Power Consumption:** Designed for battery-powered or energy-efficient applications.
- **Small Size and Low Cost:** Suitable for integration into small and cost-sensitive devices.
- **Real-Time Capabilities:** Many microcontrollers are designed for real-time applications.

Examples:

- ARM Cortex-M series: Widely used in embedded systems and IoT devices.
- Atmel AVR series: Popular among hobbyists and in industrial applications.
- Texas Instruments MSP430 series: Known for its low power consumption.
- ESP32: popular for IOT applications due to its wifi and bluetooth abilities.

The Role in CPS:

Data Acquisition and Processing: Microcontrollers process sensor data, perform signal processing, and extract relevant information.

Control Algorithms: They execute control algorithms to regulate physical processes, such as motor control and temperature control.

Communication Management: They manage communication networks, enabling data exchange between different components of the CPS.

Real-Time Control: They provide the real-time processing capabilities necessary for timely responses to events in the physical world.

Edge Computing: Microcontrollers are increasingly used in edge computing to perform local data processing and analysis, reducing the need to transmit all data to the cloud.

Importance:

- Embedded systems and microcontrollers are essential for enabling the intelligence and control capabilities of CPS.
- They allow for localized processing, reducing latency and improving system responsiveness.
- They are key to creating efficient and reliable CPS that can operate in diverse environments.

CLOUD COMPUTING AND EDGE COMPUTING:

The rise of Cloud Computing and Edge Computing has significantly transformed the landscape of Cyber-Physical Systems (CPS), enabling distributed intelligence and enhancing the capabilities of these systems. Let's break down these concepts:

Cloud Computing:

Cloud computing involves delivering computing services—including servers, storage, databases, networking, software, analytics, and intelligence—over the Internet ("the cloud"). It provides on-demand access to shared resources, eliminating the need for organizations to own and manage their own infrastructure.

Role in CPS:

- **Data Storage and Analysis:** Cloud platforms offer vast storage capacity for the large volumes of data generated by CPS, and powerful analytics tools for processing and extracting insights.
- **Centralized Control and Management:** Cloud-based applications enable remote monitoring, control, and management of distributed CPS.
- **Software Updates and Deployment:** Cloud platforms facilitate seamless software updates and deployment to CPS devices.
- **Machine Learning and AI:** Cloud providers offer machine learning and AI services that can be used to develop intelligent applications for CPS.

Advantages:

- Cloud resources can be scaled up or down as needed.
- Eliminates the need for upfront investments in infrastructure.
- Cloud services can be accessed from anywhere with an internet connection.
- Powerful computing resources.

Disadvantages:

- Communication delays can be a concern for real-time applications.
- Requires a stable internet connection.
- Data stored in the cloud may be vulnerable to cyberattacks.

Edge Computing : Edge computing involves processing data closer to the source, at the "edge" of the network, rather than sending it all to the cloud. It brings computation and data storage closer to the location where it is needed, to improve response times and save bandwidth.

Role in CPS:

Real-Time Processing: Edge devices can process sensor data in real-time, enabling rapid responses to events in the physical world.

Reduced Latency: Processing data locally minimizes communication delays, improving system responsiveness.

Bandwidth Optimization: Processing data at the edge reduces the amount of data that needs to be transmitted to the cloud.

Enhanced Reliability: Edge computing enables CPS to operate even when internet connectivity is limited or unavailable.

Increased Privacy: Sensitive data can be processed locally, reducing the risk of exposure.

Advantages:

- Low latency.
- Bandwidth efficiency.

- ◦ Improved reliability.
- ◦ Enhanced privacy.

Disadvantages:

- ◦ Limited processing power compared to the cloud.
- ◦ Increased complexity in managing distributed systems.
- ◦ Security concerns at the edge.

Distributed Intelligence

Hybrid Approach: Cloud computing and edge computing are not mutually exclusive. They can be used together to create a hybrid architecture that leverages the strengths of both. Edge devices can perform real-time processing and filter data, while the cloud can handle long-term storage, complex analytics, and machine learning tasks.

Benefits:

- Combining the real-time processing of edge computing with the powerful analytics of cloud computing.
- Distributing intelligence across the network enables CPS to adapt to changing requirements.
- Decentralized processing enhances the resilience of CPS to network outages and cyberattacks.

In essence, Cloud and Edge computing together provide the distributed intelligence needed to make modern CPS both powerful and responsive.

SYSTEM ARCHITECTURE MODELS

1. Layered Architecture

The layered architecture is built on the principle of abstraction. Each layer provides a specific set of services to the layer above it, while hiding the complexities of its internal workings. This modularity simplifies development, as teams can focus on specific layers without needing to understand the entire system. Error detection and debugging are also streamlined, as issues can often be isolated to a particular layer.

Real-World Examples:

OSI Model (Open Systems Interconnection): This seven-layer model is a foundational concept in networking, defining how communication occurs between systems. While it's a model for networking, it embodies the layered architecture concept.

Automotive Software: Modern vehicles employ layered software architectures. For instance, the lowest layer might handle sensor data acquisition, the next layer might process that data, the control layer would implement driving assistance features, and the application layer would provide user interface elements.

Building Automation Systems: HVAC, lighting, and security systems within a building might be organized in layers, with sensor data flowing upward and control signals flowing downward.

Practical Considerations:

- Define clear interfaces between layers to ensure seamless communication.
- Minimize dependencies between layers to enhance modularity.
- Carefully consider latency requirements, as data must traverse multiple layers.

2. Distributed Architecture

Distributed architectures are essential for systems that need to scale or operate in geographically dispersed environments. They emphasize redundancy and fault tolerance, as the failure of one node does not necessarily bring down the entire system. Communication protocols play a crucial role in ensuring that nodes can effectively collaborate.

Real-World Examples:

Smart Grids: Power distribution systems use distributed architectures to manage energy flow across a wide area. Sensors and control devices are distributed throughout the grid, and they communicate with each other to optimize performance.

Autonomous Vehicle Fleets: A fleet of autonomous vehicles might use a distributed architecture to share data and coordinate routes. Vehicles can communicate with each other and with infrastructure to improve traffic flow and safety.

Industrial IoT (IIoT): Manufacturing facilities use distributed architectures to connect machines and sensors across the factory floor. Data is processed locally at the edge, and aggregated data is sent to the cloud for analysis.

Blockchain Networks: A perfect example of a fully distributed system.

Practical Considerations:

- Choose appropriate communication protocols for the application (e.g., MQTT, DDS).
- Implement robust fault tolerance mechanisms to handle node failures.
- Address security concerns related to distributed data and control.

3. Hybrid Architecture: The Best of Both Worlds

Hybrid architectures offer the flexibility to tailor the system to the specific needs of the application. They allow developers to leverage the strengths of both layered and distributed models, creating a more optimized and resilient system.

Edge computing is a prime example of a hybrid architecture, where local processing is combined with cloud-based analytics.

Real-World Examples:

Smart City Platforms: A smart city platform might use a layered architecture for local traffic management and a distributed architecture for city-wide resource optimization. Edge devices would process sensor data locally, and cloud-based systems would provide city-wide analytics and control.

Advanced Robotics: A robot might use a layered architecture for its internal control systems and a distributed architecture for communication with other robots and its environment. Edge processing would be used for immediate reaction to sensor data, while cloud processing could be used for complex path planning.

Modern cloud based IOT platforms: These platforms use edge devices to collect and do intial processing of data, then use cloud based systems for long term storage, and AI processing.

By understanding these system architecture models, you can make informed decisions about how to design and implement CPS that meet the specific requirements of your applications.

DATA ACQUISITION AND PROCESSING

Data acquisition and processing form the bedrock of modern scientific inquiry, technological development, and informed decision-making. In an era characterized by an exponential surge in data generation, the ability to effectively capture, transform, and analyze raw information is paramount. This process encompasses a diverse range of techniques, from sensor-based measurements and digital signal processing to sophisticated algorithms for data cleaning and interpretation. Ultimately, the successful implementation of data acquisition and processing pipelines enables us to extract meaningful insights from complex datasets, driving innovation and facilitating a deeper understanding of the world around us.

SENSOR DATA ACQUISITION

When discussing "Sensor Data Acquisition: Techniques and Challenges," it's essential to understand the fundamental role sensors play in gathering real-world information. Here's a breakdown:

Core Concepts:

Sensors as Transducers: At their heart, sensors are transducers. This means they convert one form of energy into another. Specifically, they translate physical phenomena (like temperature, pressure, or light) into electrical signals.

Data Acquisition Systems (DAS): These systems are the bridge between the analog world of sensors and the digital world of computers. A DAS typically includes:

- **Sensors:** To capture the physical data.
- **Signal Conditioning:** To amplify, filter, or modify the sensor signal for accurate measurement.
- **Analog-to-Digital Converters (ADCs):** To convert the analog signal into digital data.
- **Computer/Software:** To store, analyze, and visualize the digital data.

Key Techniques:

Sampling: This is the process of taking measurements at discrete intervals. The sampling rate is crucial—it must be high enough to accurately capture the changes in the physical phenomenon.

Signal Conditioning: This encompasses various techniques:

- **Amplification:** Boosting weak signals.
- **Filtering:** Removing unwanted noise.
- **Linearization:** Correcting for non-linear sensor responses.

Data Logging: Storing the acquired digital data for later analysis.

Real-time Processing: Analyzing the data as it's being acquired, enabling immediate responses or control actions.

Challenges:

- **Noise:** Electrical noise can corrupt sensor signals, leading to inaccurate measurements.
- **Calibration:** Sensors can drift over time, requiring periodic calibration to maintain accuracy.
- **Environmental Factors:** Temperature, humidity, and other environmental conditions can affect sensor performance.
- **Bandwidth and Sampling Rate:** Choosing the appropriate sampling rate is critical. Too low, and data will be lost; too high, and it can overwhelm the system.

- **Sensor Selection:** Choosing the proper sensor for the specific application. Factors such as accuracy, range, and environmental withstanding need to be considered.
- **Data Volume:** With the rise of IoT and sensor networks, managing and processing vast amounts of sensor data is a significant challenge.

Sensor data acquisition is a vital process that translates real world information into a format usable by computers. But it is a complex process with many possible sources of error. Therefore, special care must be taken in all phases of the Data Acquisition process.

SIGNAL PROCESSING AND FILTERING

Signal processing and filtering are crucial steps in extracting meaningful information from raw data, especially when dealing with sensor data. Here's a detailed breakdown:

1. Signal Processing Fundamentals:

Signal processing involves analyzing, modifying, and synthesizing signals to extract useful information or improve their quality.

Domains:

- **Time Domain:** Analyzing signals as they vary over time.
- **Frequency Domain:** Analyzing the frequency components of a signal using techniques like Fourier transforms.

Objectives:

- Noise reduction.
- Feature extraction.
- Data compression.
- Signal enhancement.

2. Filtering: Noise Reduction:

To remove unwanted noise from a signal, improving its clarity and accuracy.

Types of Filters:

- **Low-Pass Filters:** Pass low-frequency signals and attenuate high-frequency signals. Useful for smoothing data and removing high-frequency noise.
- **High-Pass Filters:** Pass high-frequency signals and attenuate low-frequency signals. Useful for detecting edges or sudden changes in a signal.
- **Band-Pass Filters:** Pass signals within a specific frequency range and attenuate signals outside that range. Useful for isolating specific frequency components.
- **Band-Stop Filters (Notch Filters):** Attenuate signals within a specific frequency range and pass signals outside that range. Useful for removing specific interfering frequencies.

Digital vs. Analog Filters:

- **Digital Filters:** Implemented in software, offering flexibility and precision.
- **Analog Filters:** Implemented using electronic components, suitable for real-time applications.

3. Feature Extraction:

To identify and extract relevant characteristics or features from a signal that can be used for further analysis or decision-making.

Techniques:

- **Time-Domain Features:** Amplitude, mean, variance, standard deviation, peaks, and zero-crossing rate.
- **Frequency-Domain Features:** Frequency spectrum, spectral power, and dominant frequencies.
- **Transform-Based Features:** Features extracted using techniques like Fourier transforms, wavelet transforms, and spectrograms.

Example applications:

- Speech Recognition: Extracting features like Mel-frequency cepstral coefficients (MFCCs) to identify spoken words.
- Medical Signal Analysis: Extracting features from ECG signals to detect heart abnormalities.
- Image Processing: Extracting features like edges, corners, and textures for object recognition.

Key Considerations:

Choosing the appropriate filter type and parameters is crucial for effective noise reduction. There's often a trade-off between noise reduction and signal distortion. Aggressive filtering can remove noise but also distort important signal information. Complex signal processing algorithms can require significant computational resources.

In summary, signal processing and filtering are essential tools for extracting valuable information from noisy signals. By effectively reducing noise and extracting relevant features, we can gain deeper insights from data and improve the performance of various applications.

DATA STORAGE AND MANAGEMENT

Data storage and management are critical components of any system that handles information, and they become especially complex with the rise of "big data

1. Databases:

Traditional Databases (Relational Databases):

These organize data into tables with predefined relationships. They use Structured Query Language (SQL) for managing and querying data. They are well-suited for structured data and applications that require data integrity and consistency.

Examples: MySQL, PostgreSQL, Oracle Database.

NoSQL Databases:

These databases are designed to handle unstructured or semi-structured data, which is common in big data applications. They offer flexibility and scalability, allowing for the storage of diverse data types.

Types of NoSQL databases:

- Key-value stores (e.g., Redis)
- Document databases (e.g., MongoDB)
- Column-family stores (e.g., Cassandra)
- Graph databases (e.g., Neo4j)

2. Big Data Solutions:
Characteristics of Big Data:

- Volume: Massive amounts of data.
- Velocity: Data generated at high speed.
- Variety: Diverse data types (structured, unstructured, semi-structured).
- Veracity: Data quality and reliability.

Big Data Storage Technologies:

Centralized repositories that store vast amounts of raw data in its native format. They are designed to handle diverse data types and enable flexible data analysis. Designed for analytical purposes, storing structured data that has been processed and transformed. They are optimized for querying and reporting. Cloud platforms offer scalable and cost-effective storage solutions for big data. Examples: Amazon S3, Google Cloud Storage, Azure Blob Storage.

Big Data Management Challenges:

- **Scalability:** Handling the ever-increasing volume of data.
- **Data Integration:** Combining data from diverse sources.
- **Data Security:** Protecting sensitive data.
- **Data Governance:** Ensuring data quality and compliance.
- **Real-time Processing:** Processing data as it is generated.

The choice of data storage and management solutions depends on the specific requirements of the application, including the type of data, the volume of data, and the required performance. Cloud based solutions are becoming more and more common due to their ability to scale to meet the needs of very large datasets . In essence, effective data storage and management are crucial for extracting valuable insights from data, especially in the age of big data.

DATA ANALYTICS AND VISUALIZATION

The vast ocean of data that surrounds us, the ability to extract meaningful insights is paramount. Data analytics and visualization are the twin engines that drive this process, transforming raw, often chaotic, information into actionable knowledge. Data analytics, at its core, is the science of examining raw data to draw conclusions about that information. It involves applying various techniques to uncover hidden patterns, trends, and relationships. Data visualization, on the other hand, is the art of representing data graphically, making it easier to understand and communicate complex information.

The journey begins with **data analytics**, which acts as the analytical engine. This process involves a series of steps, starting with data cleaning and preparation. Raw data is often messy, containing errors, inconsistencies, and missing values. Data cleaning involves addressing these issues to ensure the accuracy and reliability of the analysis. Once the data is clean, various analytical techniques can be applied.

Types of Data Analytics:

- **Descriptive Analytics:** This focuses on summarizing past data to understand what has happened. It provides a snapshot of the current state of affairs, answering questions like "What were our sales figures last quarter?" or "What is the average customer age?" Descriptive analytics often involves calculating summary statistics, such as mean, median, mode, and standard deviation.
- **Diagnostic Analytics:** This aims to determine why something happened. It delves deeper into the data to identify the root

causes of observed trends or patterns. For example, "Why did sales decline in a specific region?" or "Why did customer churn increase?" Diagnostic analytics often involves using techniques like drill-down analysis, correlation analysis, and root cause analysis.

- **Predictive Analytics:** This uses historical data to forecast future trends. It leverages statistical models and machine learning algorithms to predict future outcomes, answering questions like "What are our projected sales for the next year?" or "Which customers are likely to churn?" Predictive analytics is crucial for proactive decision-making and strategic planning.
- **Prescriptive Analytics:** This goes beyond prediction to recommend actions to take based on the analysis of data. It provides actionable insights, suggesting the best course of action to achieve desired outcomes. For example, "What marketing strategies should we implement to increase sales?" or "How can we optimize our supply chain to reduce costs?" Prescriptive analytics often involves using optimization algorithms and simulation models.

The Art of Visual Communication

While data analytics provides the insights, data visualization serves as the crucial bridge between the analytical findings and human understanding. It transforms complex data into easily digestible visual representations, enabling users to quickly grasp key trends and patterns.

Data Visualization Techniques:

- **Bar Charts:** These are used to compare categorical data, displaying the frequency or magnitude of different categories.
- **Line Graphs:** These are used to show trends over time, displaying the relationship between two continuous variables.
- **Pie Charts:** These are used to show the proportions of different categories within a whole.

- **Scatter Plots:** These are used to show the relationship between two continuous variables, revealing patterns and correlations.
- **Heatmaps:** These are used to visualize data matrices, displaying the magnitude of values using color gradients.
- **Dashboards:** These are interactive displays that combine multiple visualizations, providing a comprehensive overview of key performance indicators.

Key Considerations in Data Visualization:

- The type of visualization should be chosen based on the type of data and the message being conveyed.
- Visualizations should be clear, concise, and accurate, avoiding misleading or confusing representations.
- Visualizations should be accompanied by appropriate labels, titles, and legends to provide context and facilitate understanding.
- nteractive visualizations allow users to explore data in more detail, enabling them to drill down into specific areas of interest.
- Visualizations should be designed to be accessible to all users, including those with disabilities.

Effective data visualization goes beyond simply presenting data; it tells a story. By using visual elements to highlight key trends and patterns, data visualization can engage the audience and facilitate understanding. Storytelling with data involves crafting a narrative that guides the audience through the data, highlighting key insights and driving home the message.

Applications and Impact

Data analytics and visualization are transforming industries and driving innovation across a wide range of applications.

Applications:

Data analytics and visualization are used to analyze customer behavior, optimize marketing campaigns, improve operational efficiency, and make informed business decisions. They are used to analyze patient data, identify disease patterns, improve treatment outcomes, and optimize healthcare delivery. They are used to analyze market trends, detect fraud, manage risk, and make investment decisions. They are used to analyze experimental data, visualize complex scientific phenomena, and advance scientific discovery. They are used to track student performance, identify learning gaps, and personalize learning experiences.They are used to analyze public data, monitor trends, and inform policy decisions.

Impact:

- **Improved Decision-Making:** Data analytics and visualization provide the insights needed to make informed decisions, leading to better outcomes.
- **Increased Efficiency:** They enable organizations to identify and address inefficiencies, leading to improved productivity and reduced costs.
- **Enhanced Understanding:** They facilitate understanding of complex data, enabling users to identify patterns and trends that would otherwise be hidden.
- **Data-Driven Culture:** They promote a data-driven culture, where decisions are based on evidence rather than intuition.
- **Innovation:** They drive innovation by enabling organizations to discover new insights and develop new products and services.

As data continues to grow in volume and complexity, the importance of data analytics and visualization will only increase. Advancements in artificial intelligence and machine learning are enabling more sophisticated analytical techniques, while advancements in visualization technology are creating more immersive and interactive experiences. The future of data analytics and visualization lies in the ability to seamlessly integrate these technologies, creating intelligent systems that can automatically extract insights and present them in a way that is both informative and engaging. By harnessing the power of data, we can unlock new possibilities and create a better future.

THREE

INTELLIGENT AUTOMATION IN CPS

Intelligent automation in Cyber-Physical Systems (CPS) signifies a critical evolution, moving beyond traditional, static control towards dynamic, adaptive operations. This shift is driven by the integration of artificial intelligence (AI) and machine learning (ML), enabling CPS to autonomously respond to fluctuating environments, predict and prevent failures, and optimize performance in real-time. The necessity for this intelligence stems from the increasing complexity and interconnectivity of modern CPS, which operate in dynamic and often unpredictable settings demanding adaptability and resilience. Key technologies facilitating this transformation include AI algorithms for decision-making, ML for learning and prediction, sensor fusion for comprehensive environmental awareness, edge computing for real-time responsiveness, and cloud computing for scalable data processing. Applications span diverse sectors, from smart manufacturing and autonomous vehicles to smart grids and healthcare, each leveraging intelligent automation to enhance efficiency, safety, and productivity. However, challenges such as data availability, real-time performance, security, and explainability must be addressed. Future directions point towards human-AI collaboration, federated learning for privacy, explainable AI for trust, resilient CPS designs, and the use of digital twins for simulation and optimization. Ultimately, intelligent automation is poised to revolutionize CPS, paving the way for more efficient, reliable, and adaptable systems that shape the future of our infrastructure and industries.

INTRODUCTION TO INTELLIGENT AUTOMATION

Intelligent automation marks a profound transformation in how we design, operate, and interact with systems, moving beyond the rigid, pre-programmed routines of traditional automation to embrace adaptive, learning, and decision-making capabilities. This paradigm shift is driven by the convergence of artificial intelligence (AI), machine learning (ML), and advanced computing, enabling systems to autonomously respond to dynamic environments, optimize performance, and even anticipate future needs. At its core, intelligent automation seeks to imbue machines and systems with the ability to perceive, reason, and act, mimicking human-like intelligence to achieve complex tasks with minimal human intervention. This evolution is not merely about replacing manual labor; it's about augmenting human potential, enabling us to tackle increasingly complex challenges, and unlocking new frontiers of efficiency and innovation across diverse sectors. The journey into intelligent automation begins by understanding its foundational principles, the technologies that power it, and the transformative impact it is poised to have on our world.

The foundation of intelligent automation rests upon the powerful pillars of artificial intelligence and machine learning. AI provides the cognitive framework, enabling systems to simulate human intelligence through reasoning, problem-solving, and decision-making. Machine learning, a subset of AI, empowers systems to learn from data without explicit programming, continuously improving their performance over time. These technologies are not merely theoretical concepts; they are the driving forces behind a range of applications that are reshaping industries and everyday life. AI encompasses a broad spectrum of techniques, from rule-based systems and expert systems to more advanced approaches like deep learning and reinforcement learning. Deep learning, inspired by the structure of the human brain, enables systems to learn complex patterns from vast amounts of data. Reinforcement learning, on the other hand, allows systems to learn through trial and error, optimizing their actions based on feedback from the environment.

ML algorithms are the engine that drives the learning process. Supervised learning, unsupervised learning, and reinforcement learning are the three primary categories. Supervised learning involves training models on labeled data, enabling them to make predictions or classifications. Unsupervised learning focuses on finding patterns and structures in unlabeled data, such as clustering or anomaly detection. Reinforcement learning, as mentioned earlier, enables systems to learn through interaction with the environment. Both AI and ML rely heavily on data. The quality and quantity of data are crucial for training effective models. Data acquisition, preprocessing, and management are therefore essential components of any intelligent automation system. Algorithms are the heart of AI and ML, providing the instructions for processing data and making decisions. The choice of algorithm depends on the specific task and the characteristics of the data ntelligent automation is not a futuristic concept; it is already transforming industries and shaping our daily lives. From autonomous vehicles and smart factories to personalized healthcare and intelligent homes, the applications of intelligent automation are vast and diverse.

In manufacturing, intelligent automation is enabling the development of smart factories that can optimize production processes, predict equipment failures, and adapt to changing demand. Autonomous vehicles are revolutionizing transportation, promising to improve safety, reduce congestion, and enhance mobility. AI-powered diagnostic tools, personalized treatment plans, and robotic surgery are transforming healthcare delivery.

Intelligent automation is enabling cities to optimize traffic flow, manage energy consumption, and improve public safety. Precision agriculture, powered by AI and robotics, is enabling farmers to optimize crop yields, reduce waste, and minimize environmental impact. Chatbots and virtual assistants are providing personalized and efficient customer service. The future of intelligent automation holds immense potential. As AI and ML technologies continue to advance, we can expect to see even more sophisticated and autonomous systems that can tackle increasingly complex tasks.

AUTOMATION VS. INTELLIGENT AUTOMATION:

Understanding the distinction between traditional automation and intelligent automation is crucial in today's technology-driven world. Here's a breakdown of the key differences, with a focus on the role of AI:

Traditional Automation:

Rule-Based: Traditional automation relies on pre-programmed, rigid rules. It excels at performing repetitive, predictable tasks with consistency and efficiency. "If-then" scenarios dictate the system's actions.

Limited Adaptability: These systems struggle with unexpected changes or complex, dynamic environments. They lack the ability to learn or adapt to new situations.

Focus on Repetitive Tasks: Common applications include assembly line operations, data entry, and other tasks that follow a fixed pattern.

Intelligent Automation:

AI-Driven: Intelligent automation incorporates artificial intelligence (AI) and machine learning (ML) to enable systems to learn, adapt, and make decisions. AI allows systems to analyze data, identify patterns, and respond to complex situations.

Enhanced Adaptability: AI-powered systems can adapt to changing conditions, learn from experience, and improve their performance over time. They can handle unstructured data and make decisions in uncertain environments.

Complex Decision-Making: Intelligent automation is used for tasks that require cognitive abilities, such as:

- Predictive maintenance
- Fraud detection
- Personalized customer service
- Autonomous vehicles

The Role of AI: AI is the key differentiator. It enables systems to:

- **Learn:** Through machine learning algorithms, systems can identify patterns and improve their performance.
- **Reason:** AI allows systems to analyze information and make logical decisions.
- **Perceive:** AI-powered systems can process sensory input, such as images and speech, to understand their environment.
- **Adapt:** AI enables systems to adjust their behavior in response to changing conditions.

Automation handles "what," while intelligent automation handles "why" and "how." Traditional automation is about following instructions, while intelligent automation is about making informed decisions. Traditional automation is very good at doing the same task, repeatedly, with great accuracy. Intelligent automation, is very good at adapting to changing conditions, and making decisions based on data. By integrating AI, intelligent automation expands the capabilities of traditional automation, enabling systems to handle more complex and dynamic tasks.

MACHINE LEARNING AND DEEP LEARNING FOR CPS

The convergence of computational power and real-world interaction has given rise to Cyber-Physical Systems (CPS), complex engineered systems that seamlessly blend digital and physical components.

[1] However, the increasing intricacy and data volume generated by these systems demand sophisticated analytical tools. This is where the transformative potential of Machine Learning (ML) and Deep Learning (DL) becomes evident. By enabling CPS to learn from vast datasets, these AI-driven technologies facilitate intelligent decision-making, predictive maintenance, and adaptive control, ultimately enhancing the reliability, efficiency, and autonomy of critical infrastructures and devices. In essence, ML and DL are not merely tools, but crucial enablers for the next generation of intelligent and responsive CPS.

1. CPS: Cyber-Physical Systems

Cyber-Physical Systems (CPS) are engineered systems that integrate computation, networking, and physical processes. They involve sensors, actuators, and control systems that interact with the physical world through networks.

Examples:

- Smart grids: Monitoring and controlling power distribution.
- Autonomous vehicles: Sensing the environment and making driving decisions.
- Industrial control systems: Automating manufacturing processes.
- Smart buildings: Optimizing energy usage and comfort.
- Medical devices: Monitoring patient health and delivering treatments.

Key Characteristics:

- Tight coupling between cyber (computation and communication) and physical components.
- Real-time operation and interaction with the physical environment.
- Distributed and networked nature.
- Safety-critical applications.

2. Machine Learning (ML)

Machine learning is a subfield of artificial intelligence (AI) that enables systems to learn from data without explicit programming. It involves algorithms that can identify patterns, make predictions, and improve their performance over time.

Key Concepts:

- Supervised learning: Training models on labeled data to make predictions. (e.g., classifying sensor data as normal or abnormal).
- Unsupervised learning: Discovering hidden patterns in unlabeled data. (e.g., clustering sensor data to identify anomalies).
- Reinforcement learning: Training agents to make decisions in an environment to maximize rewards. (e.g., optimizing control strategies for autonomous vehicles).

Applications in CPS:

- **Fault detection and diagnosis:** Identifying anomalies in sensor data to predict system failures.
- **Predictive maintenance:** Forecasting when equipment will need maintenance to prevent downtime.
- **Resource optimization:** Optimizing energy consumption, traffic flow, and other resources.
- **Adaptive control:** Adjusting control parameters based on real-time data.

3. Deep Learning (DL)

Deep learning is a subfield of machine learning that uses artificial neural networks with multiple layers (deep neural networks) to learn [1] complex patterns from data.

Neural networks: Interconnected nodes (neurons) that process and transmit information.

Deep neural networks (DNNs): Neural networks with many layers, enabling them to learn hierarchical representations of data.

Convolutional neural networks (CNNs): Specialized for image and video processing.

Recurrent neural networks (RNNs): Specialized for sequential data, such as time series.

Advantages in CPS:

- Ability to handle large and complex datasets.
- Automatic feature extraction, reducing the need for manual feature engineering.
- High accuracy in pattern recognition and prediction.

Applications in CPS:

- **Image and video analysis:** For autonomous vehicles, surveillance systems, and industrial inspection.
- **Time-series analysis:** For predicting equipment failures, energy consumption, and traffic flow.
- **Natural language processing (NLP):** For human-machine interaction in smart environments.
- **Complex control tasks:** Enabling more sophisticated autonomous control.

How ML and DL Enhance CPS:

ML and DL can detect anomalies and predict failures, enhancing system reliability and safety. Optimization algorithms can improve resource utilization and system performance. ML and DL enable CPS to adapt to changing conditions and make intelligent decisions. NLP and other ML techniques facilitate more natural and intuitive interactions. ML and DL can be used to predict the remaining useful life of components and systems.

In essence, Machine Learning and Deep Learning provide the tools to make Cyber-Physical Systems more intelligent, adaptable, and robust, allowing them to function more efficiently and safely in a wide range of applications.

REINFORCEMENT LEARNING FOR ADAPTIVE CONTROL

Adaptive control, the ability of a system to modify its behavior in response to changing environments or internal dynamics, is crucial for robust performance in complex and uncertain domains. [1] Traditionally, designing adaptive controllers has relied on intricate mathematical models and assumptions, often limiting their applicability. [2] However, the emergence of Reinforcement Learning (RL) presents a paradigm shift. RL, by enabling agents to learn optimal control policies through trial-and-error interaction with their environment, offers a powerful framework for developing adaptive systems that can autonomously adjust to unforeseen circumstances. [3] This introduction explores how RL's ability to learn from experience makes it an ideal candidate for tackling the challenges of adaptive control, paving the way for more resilient and intelligent systems across diverse applications.

1. Adaptive Control Fundamentals: Deep Dive

Traditional Adaptive Control:

Parameter Estimation: Traditional methods often involve identifying key parameters of the system (e.g., mass, friction) online using techniques like recursive least squares. The controller then adjusts its gains based on these estimated parameters.

Model-Based Reliance: These methods typically assume a known structure for the system's dynamics, even if the exact parameter values are unknown. This assumption simplifies analysis but limits applicability to systems with complex or uncertain dynamics.

Stability Focus: A primary concern is ensuring the stability of the closed-loop system, meaning it doesn't diverge or become unstable. Lyapunov stability theory is often employed to provide guarantees.

Challenges:

- **Nonlinearities:** Real-world systems are often nonlinear, and traditional adaptive control can struggle to handle these complexities.

- **Uncertainties**: Unmodeled dynamics, disturbances, and noise can degrade performance and even lead to instability.
- **Time-Varying Dynamics**: If the system's dynamics change rapidly, traditional methods may not be able to adapt quickly enough.

2. Reinforcement Learning's Contribution: Detailed Analysis

Model-Free Approach:

RL algorithms learn directly from experience, without needing to explicitly identify system parameters or build a model. This is crucial for systems where modeling is difficult or impossible.

Complex Systems: RL shines in situations with high-dimensional state and action spaces, where traditional modeling approaches become intractable.

Learning Through Interaction:

The agent's ability to explore the environment and learn from its mistakes is a key strength. This allows it to discover optimal strategies that might not be apparent from a model.

Reward Design: The design of the reward function is critical, as it guides the agent's learning process.

Handling Complexity:

Deep RL: Deep neural networks allow RL agents to learn complex, nonlinear mappings between states and actions.

Long-Term Goals: RL can optimize for long-term rewards, enabling it to learn control policies that maximize overall performance, even if short-term actions appear suboptimal.

3. The Synergy of RL and Adaptive Control: Bridging the Gap

Enhanced Adaptability:

RL's ability to learn online allows adaptive control systems to respond to unforeseen changes in the environment or system dynamics.

Robustness: RL can learn control policies that are robust to disturbances and noise, improving overall system resilience.

Improved Performance:
RL can discover control policies that outperform traditional methods, especially in complex or uncertain environments.

Optimization: RL can optimize for multiple objectives, such as performance, energy efficiency, and safety.

Expanded Applicability:
RL extends adaptive control to a wider range of applications, including:

- Robotics: Learning complex manipulation tasks.
- Autonomous systems: Navigating in dynamic environments.
- Smart grids: Optimizing energy distribution.

Hybrid Approaches:
Research is exploring hybrid approaches that combine the strengths of both traditional adaptive control and RL. For example, RL can be used to tune the parameters of a traditional adaptive controller.

Safety Critical Systems: Combining the proven stability of traditional methods, with the flexibility of RL is a very important goal.

4. Key Considerations: Practical Implications
Stability and Safety:

- Ensuring the stability and safety of RL-based systems is a major challenge, especially in safety-critical applications.
- Research is exploring methods for incorporating safety constraints into RL algorithms and verifying the stability of learned policies

Sample Efficiency:

- RL algorithms can require a large amount of data to learn optimal policies, which can be a bottleneck in real-world applications.

- Techniques like transfer learning and model-based RL are being explored to improve sample efficiency.

Real-Time Implementation:

- Deep RL algorithms can be computationally demanding, which can limit their applicability in real-time systems.
- Research is focused on developing efficient algorithms and hardware implementations that can meet real-time requirements.
- **Simulations:** Using simulations to train RL agents before deploying them in the real world is a very important technique.

By addressing these key considerations, researchers are paving the way for the widespread adoption of RL-based adaptive control systems in a wide range of applications.

CASE STUDIES: SMART HOMES, INDUSTRIAL AUTOMATION, AND ROBOTICS

1. Smart Homes:

Optimizing energy consumption and user comfort in a smart home with dynamic occupancy patterns and weather conditions. Rule-based systems or simple feedback controllers that respond to temperature or occupancy changes.

RL-Based Adaptive Control:

RL agents can learn individual user preferences for temperature, lighting, and appliance usage.

- **Energy Optimization:** RL can adapt HVAC (heating, ventilation, and air conditioning) systems, lighting, and appliance schedules to minimize energy consumption while maintaining user comfort.
- **Predictive Control:** RL can learn to predict future occupancy and weather patterns, enabling proactive control of home systems.

- ◦ **Adaptability:** RL can adapt to changes in user preferences, occupancy patterns, and weather conditions over time.

Example: A RL agent could learn to pre-cool a room before a user typically enters, or to adjust the heating based on real-time weather forecasts and the user's past behavior.

Benefits: Reduced energy costs, improved user comfort, and increased automation.

2. Industrial Automation:

Optimizing manufacturing processes, such as robotic assembly or chemical processing, with dynamic production demands and equipment wear. Pre-programmed control systems or PID (proportional-integral-derivative) controllers with fixed parameters.

RL-Based Adaptive Control:

- ◦ **Robotic Assembly:** RL can train robots to perform complex assembly tasks with varying part tolerances and tool wear.
- ◦ **Process Optimization:** RL can optimize process parameters, such as temperature, pressure, and flow rate, to maximize product quality and throughput.
- ◦ **Predictive Maintenance:** RL can learn to predict equipment failures based on sensor data, enabling proactive maintenance and reducing downtime.
- ◦ **Adaptive Scheduling:** RL can adapt production schedules to changing demands and equipment availability.

Example: A RL agent could learn to adjust the speed and force of a robotic arm during assembly to compensate for variations in part dimensions. Or, it can adapt a chemical process to maintain optimal yield despite fluctuations in raw material quality.

Benefits: Increased productivity, improved product quality, reduced downtime, and enhanced safety.

3. Robotics:

Enabling robots to perform complex tasks in unstructured and dynamic environments, such as autonomous navigation or manipulation. Pre-programmed motion plans or model-based control systems.

RL-Based Adaptive Control:

RL can train robots to navigate in complex environments, avoiding obstacles and adapting to changing terrain. RL can train robots to perform complex manipulation tasks, such as grasping and manipulating objects with varying shapes and sizes. RL can enable robots to learn to interact with humans in a natural and intuitive way. RL algorithms are used to teach robots how to walk, run, and adapt to many different terrains.

Example: A RL agent could train a drone to navigate through a cluttered warehouse, or a robotic arm to grasp and manipulate a variety of objects.

Benefits: Increased autonomy, improved dexterity, and enhanced adaptability.

Key Considerations Across All Case Studies:

Ensuring the safety of RL-based systems is paramount, especially in safety-critical applications. RL algorithms can require a large amount of data to learn optimal policies, which can be a challenge in real-world applications. RL algorithms must be able to operate in real-time to be effective in dynamic environments. The design of the reward function is critical, as it guides the agent's learning process. Simulators are often used to train RL agents before deploying them in the real world. Bridging the gap between simulation and reality is a key challenge.

MACHINE LEARNING FOR PREDICTIVE MAINTENANCE

In the modern industrial landscape, where operational efficiency and minimizing downtime are paramount, the traditional reactive maintenance approach—fixing equipment only after it fails—is rapidly becoming obsolete. The costs associated with unplanned downtime, including lost production, expensive repairs, and potential safety hazards, are substantial and can significantly impact a company's bottom line. Enter Predictive Maintenance (PdM), a proactive strategy that leverages data-driven insights to anticipate equipment failures before they occur. At the heart of this transformative approach lies Machine Learning (ML), a powerful set of algorithms that can analyze vast amounts of sensor data, operational logs, and historical maintenance records to identify subtle patterns and anomalies indicative of impending failures.

The evolution from reactive to predictive maintenance represents a paradigm shift. While preventative maintenance, based on scheduled inspections and component replacements, offers some improvement, it often results in unnecessary maintenance or fails to detect failures that occur between scheduled intervals. PdM, powered by ML, transcends these limitations by offering a dynamic and adaptive approach. By continuously monitoring equipment health and predicting remaining useful life (RUL), PdM enables organizations to optimize maintenance schedules, reduce costs, and enhance operational reliability.

The power of ML in PdM stems from its ability to extract meaningful information from complex and high-dimensional datasets. Sensors embedded in machinery generate a constant stream of data, capturing various parameters such as temperature, vibration, pressure, and acoustic emissions. ML algorithms can process this data in real-time, identifying subtle deviations from normal operating conditions that may signal an impending failure. This capability is particularly crucial in industries with complex machinery and stringent safety requirements, such as aerospace, manufacturing, and energy.

Furthermore, ML algorithms can learn from historical maintenance records, identifying patterns and correlations between equipment failures and operational conditions. This allows for the development of predictive models that can accurately forecast the likelihood of future failures, enabling proactive maintenance interventions. These models can be continuously refined and updated as new data becomes available, ensuring that they remain accurate and effective over time. The benefits of ML-driven PdM extend beyond cost savings and improved reliability.

By enabling proactive maintenance, organizations can also enhance safety, reduce environmental impact, and improve overall operational efficiency.

The adoption of ML for PdM is driven by several key factors. Firstly, the proliferation of low-cost sensors and the rise of the Industrial Internet of Things (IIoT) have made it possible to collect vast amounts of data from industrial equipment. Secondly, advancements in cloud computing and data analytics have provided the infrastructure and tools necessary to process and analyze this data effectively. Finally, the increasing availability of powerful ML algorithms and software libraries has made it easier for organizations to develop and deploy PdM solutions.

Different ML techniques play vital roles in PdM. Supervised learning algorithms, such as regression and classification, can be used to predict RUL and classify equipment health status based on labeled data. Unsupervised learning algorithms, such as clustering and anomaly detection, can identify unusual patterns and outliers in sensor data that may indicate impending failures. Reinforcement learning, which allows an agent to learn optimal control policies through trial and error, can be used to optimize maintenance schedules and control equipment operation to prolong its lifespan.

Implementing an effective ML-based PdM system requires a strategic approach. It involves defining clear objectives, selecting appropriate sensors and data acquisition systems, developing robust data pipelines, choosing suitable ML algorithms, and deploying the system in a production environment. Data quality is paramount, as the accuracy of the predictive models depends on the quality and completeness of the data. Furthermore, domain expertise is crucial for interpreting the results of the ML models and making informed maintenance decisions.

Despite the significant benefits, challenges remain in the widespread adoption of ML for PdM. These include data security and privacy concerns, the need for skilled data scientists and engineers, and the integration of PdM systems with existing enterprise systems. However, as technology continues to advance and organizations gain more experience with ML, these challenges are being addressed.

In conclusion, Machine Learning is revolutionizing the field of predictive maintenance, enabling organizations to move from reactive to proactive maintenance strategies. By leveraging data-driven insights, ML empowers businesses to optimize maintenance schedules, reduce costs, improve reliability, and enhance safety. As the industrial world continues to embrace digitalization and data analytics, the role of ML in PdM will only become more prominent, driving the next wave of industrial efficiency and innovation.

PREDICTIVE MAINTENANCE CONCEPTS AND BENEFITS

Predictive Maintenance (PdM) represents a paradigm shift in equipment management, moving beyond reactive and even preventative approaches to a data-driven, proactive strategy. By leveraging advanced analytical techniques, PdM aims to forecast potential equipment failures before they occur, enabling timely interventions and minimizing costly downtime. This proactive approach not only optimizes maintenance schedules and reduces expenses but also enhances operational efficiency, safety, and overall equipment reliability, making it an indispensable tool in modern industrial settings.

Core Concepts of Predictive Maintenance (PdM):

Data-Driven Approach:

Beyond sensors, operational logs, and maintenance records, data can include environmental conditions, usage patterns, and even external factors like weather. The goal is to create a comprehensive picture of equipment health. The accuracy of PdM relies heavily on data quality. This includes data completeness, consistency, and accuracy. Data cleaning and preprocessing are essential steps. Bringing data from disparate sources into a unified platform is crucial for effective analysis. This often involves data lakes or data warehouses.

Condition Monitoring:

Sensors can measure a wide range of parameters, including vibration, temperature, pressure, acoustic emissions, oil analysis, and electrical current. The choice of sensors depends on the specific equipment and failure modes. Real-time monitoring provides continuous insights, while periodic monitoring can be more cost-effective for less critical equipment. The best strategy depends on the application. Wireless sensors are becoming increasingly popular due to their ease of deployment and reduced wiring costs.

Anomaly Detection:

Traditional statistical methods, such as control charts and statistical process control (SPC), can be used to detect anomalies. More advanced techniques, such as clustering (e.g., k-means, DBSCAN), anomaly detection algorithms (e.g., isolation forest, one-class SVM), and deep learning (e.g., autoencoders), are used to detect complex and subtle anomalies. Setting correct thresholds for anomalies is very important. Too sensitive, and there will be many false positives. Not sensitive enough, and failures will be missed.

Predictive Modeling:

Regression models (e.g., linear regression, support vector regression) can be used to predict RUL. Classification models (e.g., logistic regression, decision trees, random forests) can be used to predict the likelihood of failure within a specific time window. Time-series analysis techniques (e.g., ARIMA, LSTM) are used to analyze time-dependent data and predict future trends. It is essential to validate predictive models using historical data to ensure their accuracy and reliability.

Proactive Interventions:

PdM enables the scheduling of maintenance interventions at the optimal time, minimizing downtime and costs. PdM can help optimize resource allocation, such as personnel and spare parts. PdM provides decision support for maintenance planning and execution.

2. Benefits of Predictive Maintenance: Expanding the Impact

Reduced Downtime:

- **Minimizing Production Losses:** Unplanned downtime can result in significant production losses, especially in industries with continuous processes.

- **Improved Customer Satisfaction:** Reducing downtime improves customer satisfaction by ensuring timely delivery of products and services.

Cost Savings:

- **Reduced Maintenance Costs:** PdM reduces unnecessary maintenance costs by performing maintenance only when needed.
- **Reduced Energy Consumption:** Optimizing equipment performance through PdM can reduce energy consumption.
- **Reduced Waste:** Equipment working at optimal performance reduces wasted materials.

Improved Equipment Reliability:

- **Increased Asset Utilization:** PdM increases asset utilization by maximizing the uptime of equipment.
- **Reduced Variability:** Stable and predictable production reduces variability in product quality.

Enhanced Safety:

- **Preventing Catastrophic Failures:** PdM can prevent catastrophic failures that can lead to serious accidents and injuries.
- **Environmental Protection:** Preventing equipment failures can also protect the environment by reducing the risk of leaks and spills.

Increased Operational Efficiency:

- **Optimized Production Processes:** PdM can help optimize production processes by ensuring that equipment is operating at peak performance.

- ○ **Improved Supply Chain Management:** Predictable equipment availability improves supply chain management.

Optimized Inventory Management:

- ○ **Just in Time part ordering:** Only order the parts when they are actually needed.
- ○ **Reduced storage space:** Less storage space is needed when parts are not stored for long periods of time.

Extended Asset Lifespan:

- ○ **Reduced Wear and Tear:** Proactive maintenance reduces wear and tear on equipment, extending its lifespan.
- ○ **Improved Resale Value:** Well-maintained equipment has a higher resale value.

Data-Driven Decision Making:

- ○ **Improved Equipment Design:** Analyzing failure data can provide insights into equipment design flaws and lead to improvements.
- ○ **Optimized Operational Procedures:** Data can be used to optimize operational procedures and improve overall efficiency.
- ○ **Performance Benchmarking:** Data can be used to benchmark equipment performance against industry standards.

By expanding on these concepts, we can better understand the transformative potential of Predictive Maintenance in modern industrial settings.

DATA-DRIVEN FAULT DETECTION AND DIAGNOSIS

Data-driven fault detection and diagnosis (FDD) is a crucial aspect of maintaining the reliability and efficiency of complex systems. It involves using data analysis techniques to identify and pinpoint the causes of malfunctions or deviations from normal operating conditions. Let's break down this concept:

Data-Driven Approach:

Reliance on Data: Instead of relying solely on physical models or expert knowledge, data-driven FDD leverages the information contained within sensor readings, operational logs, and other data sources. This approach is particularly valuable for systems where precise physical models are unavailable or too complex to develop.

Data Acquisition: The foundation of data-driven FDD is the collection of relevant data. This requires sensors that can capture key parameters of the system's operation. Data acquisition systems must be robust and reliable to ensure accurate and consistent data collection.

Data Preprocessing: Raw data often contains noise, missing values, and inconsistencies. Data preprocessing techniques are used to clean and prepare the data for analysis. This may involve filtering, normalization, feature extraction, and dimensionality reduction.

Fault Detection:

Fault detection focuses on identifying deviations from normal operating patterns. This can be achieved through statistical methods, machine learning algorithms, or a combination of both. The goal is to detect when a fault has occurred, even if the specific cause is unknown.

Techniques:

- **Statistical Process Control (SPC):** Monitoring statistical parameters of the data to detect deviations from normal distributions.
- **Threshold-Based Detection:** Setting thresholds for key parameters and triggering alarms when the thresholds are exceeded.

Machine Learning (ML):

- **Anomaly Detection Algorithms:** Algorithms like Isolation Forest, One-Class SVM, and autoencoders can identify outliers in the data.
- **Classification Models:** Models trained to classify data as normal or faulty.

- **Early Detection:**

  ○ Early detection of faults is crucial for preventing catastrophic failures and minimizing downtime.

Fault Diagnosis:

Once a fault has been detected, fault diagnosis aims to identify the specific cause of the malfunction. This involves analyzing the data to determine the location and nature of the fault.

Techniques:

- **Rule-Based Systems:** Using expert knowledge to create rules that map symptoms to causes.
- **Model-Based Diagnosis:** Comparing observed behavior with expected behavior from a system model.

Machine Learning (ML):

  ▪ **Classification Models:** Models trained to classify faults into specific categories.
  ▪ **Clustering Algorithms:** Grouping similar fault patterns to identify common causes.
  ▪ **Causal Inference:** Techniques to identify causal relationships between variables and determine the root cause of faults.

Root Cause Analysis: The ultimate goal of fault diagnosis is to perform root cause analysis, which involves identifying the underlying cause of the fault and taking corrective action to prevent recurrence.

Benefits of Data-Driven FDD:

Early detection and diagnosis of faults reduce the risk of equipment failures and improve overall system reliability. Quick identification and resolution of faults minimize downtime and production losses. Preventing major failures and optimizing maintenance schedules reduce maintenance costs. Early detection of faults can prevent accidents and improve safety. Optimizing equipment performance through FDD improves overall efficiency. Enables a shift from reactive to proactive maintenance strategies. Provides valuable data that can be used to improve equipment design and operational procedures. In essence, data-driven fault detection and diagnosis empowers organizations to proactively manage equipment health, minimize risks, and optimize performance by leveraging the power of data analysis and machine learning.

REMAINING USEFUL LIFE (RUL) PREDICTION

Estimating the Remaining Useful Life (RUL) of critical equipment has emerged as a cornerstone of modern predictive maintenance strategies. By moving beyond reactive or time-based maintenance, RUL prediction leverages data-driven techniques to anticipate equipment failures, enabling proactive interventions that minimize downtime, optimize resource allocation, and enhance overall operational efficiency. This proactive approach not only translates to significant cost savings but also fosters a safer and more reliable operational environment, making RUL prediction an indispensable tool for industries seeking to maximize asset utilization and maintain a competitive edge.

Understanding RUL: Expanding the Context

It's important to note that RUL is probabilistic, not deterministic. It's an estimation with a degree of uncertainty. The "end of operational life" can be defined in various ways (e.g., functional failure, performance degradation below a threshold, economic obsolescence).

Importance:

- **Risk Mitigation:** RUL prediction helps quantify and manage the risk of unexpected failures, allowing for proactive risk mitigation strategies.
- **Decision Support:** RUL predictions provide valuable information for decision-making regarding maintenance scheduling, spare parts procurement, and asset replacement.
- **Life Cycle Management:** RUL prediction is a key component of asset life cycle management, enabling organizations to optimize the use of their assets throughout their lifespan.

2. Data and Techniques: Deepening the Details

Data Acquisition: Combining data from different sensor types (e.g., vibration, temperature, oil analysis) can provide a more comprehensive picture of equipment health. Processing sensor data at the edge (near the source) can reduce latency and bandwidth requirements.

Data Preprocessing: Techniques like wavelet transforms and Fourier transforms can extract features from vibration and acoustic data that are indicative of fault conditions. Techniques like imputation and interpolation can be used to handle missing data points. Creating synthetic data can help improve the performance of machine learning models, especially when limited failure data is available.

Modeling Techniques:

Physics-Based Models: These models can incorporate factors like fatigue, wear, and corrosion. They can be used to simulate the degradation process and predict RUL.

Data-Driven Models:

- Feature Engineering Importance: The quality of features extracted from the data has a significant impact on the accuracy of RUL predictions.

- Deep Learning Details: CNNs can be used to analyze image-like representations of sensor data. RNNs, especially LSTMs, are well-suited for capturing long-term dependencies in time-series data.
- Transfer Learning: Using pretrained models can reduce the amount of data required for training.
- Ensemble Models: Combining multiple models can improve prediction accuracy and robustness.
- Probabilistic RUL Prediction: Providing a probability distribution of the RUL, rather than a single point estimate, is very useful.

RUL Prediction Process:

Feature Engineering: Domain expertise is crucial for selecting and extracting relevant features. Automated feature engineering techniques can also be used.

Model Validation: Cross-validation techniques are used to evaluate the model's performance on unseen data. Metrics like root mean squared error (RMSE) and mean absolute error (MAE) are used to assess prediction accuracy. Providing confidence intervals for RUL predictions is very important.

Continuous Monitoring: Online learning techniques can be used to update the model in real-time. Feedback loops can be used to incorporate maintenance information into the model.

Challenges:

Different operating conditions, environmental factors, and usage patterns can affect equipment degradation. Robust models are needed to handle this variability. Multiple failure modes can occur, each with its own degradation pattern. Models need to be able to identify and distinguish between different failure modes. Quantifying and managing uncertainty is crucial for making informed decisions. Probabilistic RUL predictions and confidence intervals can help address this challenge. Deep learning models can be computationally expensive to train and deploy. Edge computing can help.

Benefits:

- RUL predictions provide valuable information for making informed decisions about maintenance, operations, and asset management.
- Proactive maintenance strategies can improve operational efficiency, reduce costs, and enhance competitiveness.
- Optimizing asset utilization and reducing waste can contribute to sustainability goals.

By expanding on these points, we can gain a deeper appreciation for the value and complexity of RUL prediction.

IMPLEMENTATION STRATEGIES AND CHALLENGES

The successful implementation of data-driven solutions like Predictive Maintenance (PdM) or Remaining Useful Life (RUL) prediction hinges on well-defined strategies and a clear understanding of the inherent challenges. While the potential benefits are substantial, transitioning from traditional maintenance practices to a data-centric approach requires careful planning, robust infrastructure, and a commitment to overcoming obstacles related to data quality, technological integration, and organizational change. This section will explore the key implementation strategies necessary for realizing the full potential of these technologies, while also addressing the common challenges that organizations may encounter along the way.

Implementation Strategies:

Defining Clear Objectives and Scope: Start with a well-defined problem statement. Identify specific equipment or processes where PdM/RUL prediction will have the greatest impact. Set measurable goals (e.g., reduce downtime by X%, decrease maintenance costs by Y%).Conduct a pilot project on a small subset of equipment to validate the approach and demonstrate ROI before scaling up.

Data Infrastructure and Acquisition: Establish a robust data infrastructure to collect, store, and process data from various sources (sensors, operational logs, maintenance records). Ensure data quality and consistency. Invest in reliable sensors and data acquisition systems. Implement a data lake or data warehouse to centralize data. Establish data governance policies to ensure data quality.

Feature Engineering and Model Development: Extract relevant features from raw data that correlate with equipment health and RUL. Select appropriate machine learning algorithms based on the data and objectives.Leverage domain expertise to identify relevant features. Experiment with different machine learning models and techniques. Validate models using historical data and performance metrics.

Integration with Existing Systems: Seamlessly integrate PdM/RUL prediction systems with existing enterprise systems (e.g., ERP, CMMS). Use APIs and data integration tools to connect systems. Ensure data synchronization and compatibility. Create workflows to send alerts and maintenance requests to the correct personnel.

Change Management and Training: Address organizational resistance to change and provide adequate training to personnel on how to use the new system. Involve stakeholders from all departments in the implementation process. Provide comprehensive training on data interpretation and maintenance procedures. Foster a data-driven culture.

Continuous Monitoring and Improvement: Continuously monitor the performance of the PdM/RUL prediction system and make adjustments as needed. Establish key performance indicators (KPIs) to track system performance. Regularly update models with new data. Conduct periodic reviews and audits.

II. Challenges:

Data Quality and Availability: Insufficient or poor-quality data can significantly impact the accuracy of PdM/RUL prediction models.

Challenges:

- Missing data, noisy data, and inconsistent data.

- Lack of historical failure data.
- Data silos and lack of data integration.

Model Complexity and Accuracy: Selecting the right machine learning model and tuning its parameters can be challenging.
Challenges:

- Overfitting and underfitting of models.
- Difficulty in interpreting complex models.
- The inherent uncertainty of predicting future failures.

Integration with Legacy Systems: Integrating new PdM/RUL prediction systems with legacy systems can be complex and expensive.
Challenges:

- Compatibility issues and data format differences.
- Lack of APIs and integration tools.
- Security concerns.

Organizational Resistance to Change: Employees may resist adopting new technologies and processes.
Challenges:

- Lack of understanding and trust in data-driven solutions.
- Fear of job displacement.
- Resistance to changing established workflows.

Cost and ROI: Implementing PdM/RUL prediction systems can be expensive, and it may take time to realize the full ROI.
Challenges:

- High upfront costs for sensors, software, and infrastructure.

- Difficulty in quantifying the benefits of PdM/RUL prediction.
- Proving value to stakeholders.

Cybersecurity: As systems become more connected, cybersecurity risks increase.
Challenges:

- Protecting sensitive data.
- Preventing unauthorized access to systems.
- Responding to cyberattacks.

Scalability: Scaling a pilot program to an enterprise-wide implementation can be difficult.
Challenges:

- Handling large volumes of data.
- Maintaining system performance.
- Managing a distributed system.

CONTROL AND OPTIMIZATION WITH AI

The integration of Artificial Intelligence (AI) into control and optimization systems is revolutionizing how we manage and enhance complex processes. By harnessing the power of machine learning, deep learning, and reinforcement learning, AI enables systems to adapt, learn, and improve autonomously, moving beyond the limitations of traditional rule-based or model-dependent approaches. This paradigm shift allows for the creation of intelligent systems capable of optimizing performance, resource utilization, and efficiency in dynamic and uncertain environments, paving the way for a new era of intelligent automation.

ADAPTIVE CONTROL SYSTEMS

In an era characterized by increasing complexity and uncertainty, the ability of systems to adapt and respond effectively to dynamic environments is paramount. Traditional control systems, often designed with fixed parameters based on idealized models, struggle to maintain optimal performance when faced with unforeseen changes. These changes can manifest as variations in operating conditions, shifts in system parameters due to wear and tear, or external disturbances that were not accounted for during design. To address these limitations, Adaptive Control Systems have emerged as a critical technology, enabling systems to learn and adjust their behavior in real-time.

The core principle behind Adaptive Control is the continuous monitoring of system performance and the subsequent adjustment of control parameters to maintain desired outcomes. This dynamic adaptation is achieved through various techniques that allow the system to learn from its interactions with the environment and refine its control strategies over time. Unlike traditional control methods that rely on pre-defined models and parameters, adaptive control systems employ online estimation and learning algorithms to identify and compensate for changes in the system or environment. This capability is particularly vital in applications where precise models are difficult to obtain or where operating conditions are subject to significant variations. Adaptive control systems can be broadly categorized into several types, including model reference adaptive control (MRAC), self-tuning regulators (STR), and gain scheduling. MRAC compares the system's output to a desired reference model and adjusts the controller parameters to minimize the error. STR, on the other hand, estimates the system parameters online and uses these estimates to tune the controller. Gain scheduling involves switching between pre-designed controllers based on measured operating conditions. Each approach offers unique advantages and is suitable for different types of systems and applications.

The benefits of adaptive control extend beyond improved performance and stability. By enabling systems to operate effectively in dynamic environments, adaptive control can lead to reduced maintenance costs, extended equipment lifespan, and enhanced safety. For example, in aerospace applications, adaptive control systems can compensate for changes in aircraft aerodynamics due to varying flight conditions or damage. In industrial automation, these systems can optimize production processes by adapting to changes in raw material quality or equipment wear. The implementation of adaptive control systems, however, comes with its own set of challenges. One of the primary challenges is ensuring the stability and robustness of the adaptive control loop. Since the control parameters are continuously adjusted, it is crucial to guarantee that the system remains stable and does not exhibit undesirable oscillations or instability. This requires careful design of the adaptation algorithms and rigorous analysis of the system's stability properties. Another challenge is the computational complexity of adaptive control algorithms. Online estimation and learning can be computationally intensive, especially for complex systems with high-dimensional state spaces. This can limit the applicability of adaptive control in real-time applications where computational resources are constrained. Advancements in computing hardware and efficient algorithm design are crucial for overcoming these limitations.

Data quality and availability also play a significant role in the performance of adaptive control systems. Accurate and reliable data are essential for online parameter estimation and adaptation. Sensor noise, measurement errors, and data latency can degrade the performance of adaptive control loops. Therefore, robust data preprocessing and filtering techniques are necessary to ensure the quality of the data used for adaptation. The integration of machine learning techniques, particularly reinforcement learning, is further enhancing the capabilities of adaptive control systems. Reinforcement learning enables systems to learn optimal control policies through trial and error, without requiring explicit models of the system or environment. This approach is particularly promising for applications where the system dynamics are highly uncertain or where the control objectives are complex.

Looking ahead, the development of more sophisticated adaptive control algorithms, coupled with advancements in sensing, computing, and machine learning, will continue to drive innovation in various domains. From autonomous vehicles and robotics to smart grids and healthcare, adaptive control systems are poised to play a pivotal role in enabling the next generation of intelligent and resilient automated systems. By continuously learning and adapting to changes, these systems will ensure optimal performance, safety, and efficiency in an increasingly dynamic and unpredictable world.

Real-Time Adjustment :

Adaptive control systems continuously monitor the system's performance and adjust their control parameters based on the observed behavior. This differs from traditional control systems, which rely on fixed parameters that are designed for a specific operating point.

Why Adaptive Control is Needed:

Many real-world systems have uncertainties in their dynamics, making it difficult to design fixed controllers that perform well under all conditions. Equipment wear, environmental changes, and other factors can cause system parameters to change over time. Many systems exhibit nonlinear behavior, which can be difficult to model and control with traditional linear control techniques. Unpredictable disturbances can affect the system's performance.

Types of Adaptive Control:

- **Model Reference Adaptive Control (MRAC):** The system's output is compared to the output of a desired reference model. The controller parameters are adjusted to minimize the error between the system's output and the reference model's output.
- **Self-Tuning Regulators (STR):** The system parameters are estimated online. The controller parameters are then tuned based on the estimated system parameters.
- **Gain Scheduling:** The controller gains are switched between pre-designed values based on measured operating conditions. This is a simpler form of adaptive control that is often used when the operating conditions can be easily measured.

- **Reinforcement Learning Based Adaptive Control:** The control system learns through trial and error, by interacting with the environment. It recieves rewards for desired actions, and penalties for undesired actions. This is very powerful in systems where creating a model is very difficult, or impossible.

4. Key Components:

- **Identification Mechanism:** Estimates the system parameters or identifies changes in the system dynamics.
- **Adaptation Mechanism:** Adjusts the controller parameters based on the identified changes.
- **Control Law:** Determines the control actions based on the adjusted controller parameters.

5. Applications:

- **Aerospace:** Controlling aircraft and spacecraft in varying atmospheric conditions.
- **Robotics:** Enabling robots to adapt to changing environments and perform complex tasks.
- **Process Control:** Optimizing industrial processes with varying raw material quality and operating conditions.
- **Automotive:** Improving vehicle stability and handling in varying road conditions.
- **Smart Grids:** Adjusting to the dynamic nature of power consumption and generation.

6. Challenges:

- Ensuring the stability of the adaptive control loop.
- Designing controllers that are robust to noise and disturbances.
- Implementing adaptive control algorithms in real-time.
- Accurate and reliable data is essential for parameter estimation.

- Ensuring that the system converges to the desired operating point.

OPTIMIZATION ALGORITHMS:

Optimization algorithms are the workhorses behind countless technological advancements, from machine learning models to complex engineering designs. In essence, they are computational procedures designed to find the best possible solution to a problem, given a set of constraints and objectives. These algorithms navigate through a vast solution space, iteratively refining potential solutions until an optimal or near-optimal outcome is achieved. The need for efficient and effective optimization is ubiquitous, as it underpins our ability to maximize efficiency, minimize costs, and enhance performance across diverse fields. This exploration will delve into the core concepts and methodologies of optimization algorithms, highlighting their pivotal role in solving real-world challenges and driving innovation.

Core Concepts:

Objective Function: This is the heart of any optimization problem. It's a mathematical expression that quantifies what you want to achieve.

Example: In a manufacturing setting, the objective function could be the total cost of producing a certain number of units, where the cost depends on factors like raw material prices, labor costs, and energy consumption.

Maximization vs. Minimization: Some problems aim to find the highest possible value (e.g., maximizing profit), while others aim to find the lowest possible value (e.g., minimizing error).

Decision Variables:

These are the controllable factors that you can adjust to influence the objective function.

Example: In the manufacturing example, decision variables could be the quantity of raw materials to purchase, the number of workers to hire, or the production speed of machines.

Constraints:

These are limitations or restrictions that must be satisfied by the decision variables.

Example: Constraints could include budget limitations, production capacity limits, or quality requirements.

Types: Constraints can be equality constraints (e.g., the total production must equal a specific number) or inequality constraints (e.g., the production cost must be below a certain threshold).

Solution Space:

This is the set of all possible combinations of decision variable values that satisfy the constraints.

Visualization: In simple problems with two or three decision variables, the solution space can be visualized as a region in a graph. In more complex problems, it can be a high-dimensional space.

Optimal Solution:

This is the point within the solution space that yields the best possible value of the objective function.

Global vs. Local Optima: A global optimum is the best solution overall, while a local optimum is the best solution within a limited region of the solution space.

**2. Types of Optimization Algorithms: Detailed Explanation
Classical Optimization Algorithms:**

- Deals with problems where the objective function and constraints are linear. A common algorithm for solving linear programming problems. Resource allocation, production planning, transportation.
- Handles problems where the objecttive function or constraints are nonlinear. Gradient-based methods, sequential quadratic programming (SQP). Chemical process optimization, structural design.

Gradient Descent:

An iterative algorithm that moves towards the minimum of a function by taking steps in the direction of the negative gradient. A crucial parameter that controls the size of the steps. Training neural networks, curve fitting.

Newton's Method:

Uses the second derivative of the function to find the minimum, which can lead to faster convergence than gradient descent. Requires calculating the Hessian matrix, which can be computationally expensive. Optimization problems with smooth and well-behaved functions.

Heuristic and Metaheuristic Optimization Algorithms:

- **Genetic Algorithms:**

  - Mimic the process of natural selection, using concepts like selection, crossover, and mutation.
  - **Population-Based:** Works with a population of candidate solutions.
  - **Applications:** Combinatorial optimization, feature selection, parameter tuning.

- **Simulated Annealing:**

  - Explores the solution space by accepting both better and worse solutions, with a probability that decreases over time.
  - **Temperature Parameter:** Controls the probability of accepting worse solutions.
  - **Applications:** Traveling salesman problem, circuit design.

- **Particle Swarm Optimization (PSO):**

  - Simulates the social behavior of a swarm of particles, where each particle moves through the solution space based on its own experience and the experience of the swarm.
  - **Velocity and Position:** Particles have a velocity and position, which are updated iteratively.

- **Applications:** Function optimization, neural network training.

- **Ant Colony Optimization (ACO):**

  - Mimics the foraging behavior of ants, where ants deposit pheromone trails to guide the search for optimal paths.
  - **Pheromone Trails:** Used to represent the desirability of paths.
  - **Applications:** Traveling salesman problem, routing problems.

3. Applications: Real-World Scenarios

Machine Learning: Optimizing the weights and biases of neural networks to minimize the error between predicted and actual outputs. Hyperparameter tuning to find the best settings for machine learning models.

Engineering Design: Optimizing the shape and dimensions of structures to minimize weight or maximize strength. Designing efficient circuits with minimal power consumption.

Operations Research: Scheduling production to minimize costs and meet deadlines. Optimizing logistics and transportation routes to minimize delivery times. Resource allocation to maximize efficiency.

Finance: Building investment portfolios that maximize returns and minimize risk. Optimizing trading strategies.

Robotics: Planning optimal paths for robots to navigate through complex environments. Controlling robot movements to perform tasks efficiently.

Supply Chain Management: Optimizing inventory levels to minimize storage costs and prevent stockouts. Optimizing transportation and distribution networks to minimize costs and delivery times.

4. Key Considerations:

The choice of algorithm depends on the problem's characteristics (e.g., linearity, size, constraints). Some algorithms are better suited for specific types of problems. Ensuring that the algorithm finds a solution within a reasonable time. Some algorithms may converge slowly or not at all. Balancing the accuracy of the solution with the computational cost of the algorithm. Some algorithms are computationally expensive, especially for large-scale problems. Many algorithms can get stuck in local optima, which are not the best solutions overall. Metaheuristic algorithms are often used to address this issue. Properly setting starting conditions can help to avoid local optima.

MULTI-AGENT SYSTEMS

Multi-Agent Systems (MAS) represent a paradigm shift in how we approach complex problem-solving, moving away from centralized control to distributed, collaborative decision-making.At their core, MAS consist of multiple autonomous entities, or "agents," that interact within a shared environment. [2] Each agent possesses its own set of goals, capabilities, and knowledge, and they work together, either cooperatively or competitively, to achieve a common objective or individual aims within a shared space. [2] This distributed nature allows MAS to tackle problems that are inherently complex, dynamic, or geographically dispersed, where centralized control would be impractical or inefficient. [3] The strength of MAS lies in their ability to leverage the collective intelligence and diverse perspectives of individual agents, enabling them to adapt to changing conditions, handle uncertainties, and solve problems that would be intractable for single-agent systems. [4] From coordinating traffic flow in smart cities to managing complex supply chains or deploying swarms of robots for exploration, MAS offer a powerful framework for addressing real-world challenges that demand collaborative and adaptive solutions. [2] The key to their effectiveness lies in the design of agent architectures, communication protocols, and coordination mechanisms that facilitate efficient information exchange and decision-making among the agents, ultimately driving the system towards its desired outcome.

Core Concepts:

Agents: Autonomous entities with their own goals, beliefs, capabilities, and plans. They can perceive their environment, reason about it, and act upon it. They can be homogeneous (all agents are the same) or heterogeneous (agents have different capabilities).

Environment: The shared space in which agents operate. It can be static or dynamic, discrete or continuous, and deterministic or stochastic.

Interaction: Agents communicate and coordinate with each other to achieve their goals. This can involve direct communication, shared information, or indirect influence through actions in the environment.

Coordination: Agents work together to avoid conflicts and achieve a common objective. Coordination mechanisms can be centralized or distributed, explicit or implicit.

Collaboration: Agents cooperate to achieve a shared goal, often by sharing resources and information. This is a key component to many successful multi agent systems.

Key Characteristics:

- Decision-making is spread across multiple agents, rather than concentrated in a single entity.
- Agents can make decisions independently, without constant supervision.
- MAS can adapt to changing environments and unexpected events.
- MAS can handle large and complex problems by adding more agents.
- If one agent fails, the system can continue to operate with the remaining agents.

Types of Interactions:

- **Cooperation:** Agents work together to achieve a common goal.

- **Competition:** Agents compete for resources or to achieve conflicting goals.
- **Coordination:** Agents synchronize their actions to avoid conflicts and achieve efficiency.

Applications:

Robotics: Swarm robotics, where multiple robots work together to perform tasks. Collaborative robots in manufacturing.

Traffic Management: Optimizing traffic flow in smart cities.

Supply Chain Management: Coordinating the flow of goods and information between different entities.

Distributed Sensor Networks: Collecting and processing data from multiple sensors.

Challenges:

- Designing efficient and reliable communication protocols.
- Developing effective coordination mechanisms to avoid conflicts.
- Handling situations where agents have conflicting goals.
- Ensuring that agents are trustworthy and that the system is secure.
- The system as a whole can exhibit unexpected behaviors.

In essence, Multi-Agent Systems offer a powerful approach to solving complex problems by leveraging the collective intelligence and distributed decision-making of multiple agents.

REAL-TIME CONTROL AND SCHEDULING

Real-time control and scheduling are critical aspects of systems that must respond to events within strict time constraints. These systems are prevalent in various applications, from industrial automation and robotics to aerospace and medical devices. Let's break down these concepts:

1. Real-Time Control: Real-time control involves systems that monitor and manipulate physical processes in a timely manner. The correctness of the system depends not only on the logical result of the computation but also on the time at which the result is produced.

Key Characteristics:

- ○ **Time Constraints:** Tasks must be completed within specific deadlines.
- ○ **Predictability:** The system's behavior must be predictable and deterministic.
- ○ **Responsiveness:** The system must react quickly to external events.
- ○ **Reliability:** The system must be robust and fault-tolerant.

Types of Real-Time Systems:

- **Hard Real-Time:** Missing a deadline can lead to catastrophic consequences (e.g., aircraft control, medical devices).
- **Soft Real-Time:** Missing a deadline degrades performance but does not cause system failure (e.g., multimedia streaming).
- **Firm Real-Time:** Missing a deadline renders the result useless, but does not cause catastrophic failure (e.g., some telecommunications).

Techniques:

1. **Control Theory:** Using feedback loops and control algorithms to maintain desired system behavior.
2. **Real-Time Operating Systems (RTOS):** Providing scheduling and resource management capabilities to meet time constraints.
3. **Priority-Based Scheduling:** Assigning priorities to tasks to ensure that critical tasks are executed first.
4. **Interrupt Handling:** Responding quickly to external events.

2. Real-Time Scheduling: Real-time scheduling involves allocating computational resources (e.g., CPU time) to tasks in a way that satisfies their time constraints. The goal is to ensure that all critical tasks meet their deadlines.

- ○ **Tasks:** Units of work that need to be executed.
- ○ **Deadlines:** Time constraints associated with tasks.
- ○ **Scheduling Algorithms:** Algorithms used to determine the order in which tasks are executed.

Scheduling Algorithms:

- ○ **Rate-Monotonic Scheduling (RMS):** Assigns priorities based on task periods (shorter period = higher priority).
- ○ **Earliest Deadline First (EDF):** Assigns priorities based on task deadlines (earlier deadline = higher priority).
- ○ **Least Laxity First (LLF):** Assigns priorities based on task laxity (smaller laxity = higher priority). Laxity is the time remaining until a task's deadline, minus its remaining execution time.
- ○ **Fixed Priority Scheduling:** Tasks are assigned a static priority.
- ○ **Dynamic Priority Scheduling:** task priorities can change during runtime.

Challenges:

- ○ Allocating CPU time, memory, and other resources to tasks.
- ○ Handling tasks that depend on each other.
- ○ Managing situations where the system is overloaded with tasks.
- ○ variability in the time that tasks start and stop.
- ○ The overhead associated with switching between tasks.

3. Applications:

- **Industrial Automation:** Controlling manufacturing processes, robots, and other equipment.

- **Aerospace:** Controlling aircraft, spacecraft, and satellites.
- **Automotive:** Controlling engine management systems, anti-lock braking systems, and autonomous driving systems.
- **Medical Devices:** Controlling pacemakers, ventilators, and other life-critical devices.
- **Telecommunications:** Handling real-time data transmission and processing.
- **Multimedia:** Streaming audio and video with minimal latency.
- **Gaming:** Rendering graphics and handling game logic in real time.

4. Importance:

- Real-time control is crucial for safety-critical systems, where failures can have severe consequences.
- Real-time scheduling optimizes resource utilization and improves system performance.
- Real-time systems are designed to be robust and fault-tolerant.
- For customer facing products, real time systems create better user experiences.

FOUR

SECURITY AND RESILIENCE IN CPS

Cyber-Physical Systems (CPS), the intricate fusion of computational and physical processes, have become the backbone of modern infrastructure, driving innovations across domains like smart grids, autonomous vehicles, and industrial automation. However, this convergence also introduces a new frontier of vulnerabilities, where cyber threats can have devastating physical consequences. As CPS become increasingly interconnected and reliant on data-driven decision-making, the imperative for robust security and resilience has never been more critical. Traditional cybersecurity measures, designed for isolated IT systems, are often inadequate for the unique challenges posed by CPS. These systems operate in real-time, interact directly with the physical world, and often involve safety-critical operations. A successful cyberattack can not only disrupt operations but also cause physical damage, endanger human lives, and undermine public trust. Therefore, a comprehensive approach to security and resilience is essential, encompassing threat modeling, vulnerability assessment, intrusion detection, and recovery strategies tailored to the specific characteristics of CPS. This exploration will delve into the multifaceted aspects of securing and building resilience into CPS, examining the unique threats they face and the strategies necessary to mitigate those risks, ensuring the continued safe and reliable operation of these vital systems.

Building resilience in CPS goes beyond simply preventing attacks; it also involves ensuring that systems can withstand and recover from disruptions, whether caused by malicious actors, natural disasters, or technical failures. This requires a holistic approach that considers the entire lifecycle of the system, from design and development to deployment and maintenance. Redundancy, diversity, and adaptability are key principles in building resilient CPS. Redundant components and communication pathways can ensure that critical functions continue to operate even if some parts of the system are compromised. Diverse hardware and software platforms can reduce the risk of single points of failure. Adaptability allows the system to adjust its behavior in response to changing conditions, mitigating the impact of unexpected events.

Furthermore, a culture of security and resilience must be fostered at all levels of an organization. This includes training personnel on cybersecurity best practices, establishing clear incident response procedures, and promoting collaboration between IT and operational technology (OT) teams. Security must be embedded into the design of CPS, rather than being an afterthought.

This involves implementing secure coding practices, conducting thorough security testing, and regularly updating software and firmware. Continuous monitoring and threat intelligence are also essential for detecting and responding to cyberattacks in real-time. By combining robust security measures with proactive resilience strategies, organizations can ensure that their CPS remain safe, reliable, and trustworthy, even in the face of evolving threats. The future of our critical infrastructure depends on our ability to effectively address the security and resilience challenges posed by CPS, safeguarding the interconnected world we rely on.

CYBERSECURITY THREATS AND VULNERABILITIES

In an increasingly interconnected digital landscape, cybersecurity threats and vulnerabilities pose a significant and ever-evolving risk to individuals, organizations, and critical infrastructure. The rapid proliferation of digital technologies, coupled with the growing sophistication of malicious actors, has created a complex threat environment where sensitive data, operational systems, and even physical safety can be compromised. Understanding the diverse range of cyber threats—from malware and phishing to sophisticated ransomware attacks and state-sponsored intrusions—is crucial for developing effective defense strategies. Similarly, identifying and mitigating vulnerabilities in software, hardware, and network configurations is essential to prevent exploitation by adversaries. This exploration will delve into the multifaceted nature of cybersecurity threats and vulnerabilities, highlighting their impact and the critical need for proactive security measures to safeguard our digital assets and maintain trust in the interconnected world.

ATTACK VECTORS IN CPS

Cyber-Physical Systems (CPS) present a unique challenge in cybersecurity due to their tight coupling of computational and physical components. This integration introduces a broader attack surface, making CPS vulnerable to a variety of attack vectors that span hardware, software, and network domains. Let's expand on these attack vectors:

Hardware Attack Vectors:

Physical Tampering:

Direct access to hardware components allows attackers to manipulate or replace them. This can involve inserting malicious chips, modifying firmware, or physically disrupting sensors and actuators.

Examples:

- Inserting rogue devices into industrial control systems to manipulate processes.
- Tampering with sensors in autonomous vehicles to provide false readings.

- Hardware Trojans: Malicious circuitry embedded within integrated circuits during manufacturing.

Impact: Can lead to physical damage, process disruption, and data manipulation.

Side-Channel Attacks:

Exploiting information leaked from hardware during operation, such as power consumption, electromagnetic emissions, or timing variations.

Examples:

- Extracting cryptographic keys by analyzing power consumption patterns.
- Inferring sensitive data by monitoring electromagnetic emissions.

Impact: Can compromise sensitive information and enable further attacks.

Fault Injection Attacks:

Intentionally introducing faults into hardware to disrupt its operation or bypass security mechanisms.

Examples:

- Voltage glitching to induce errors in microcontrollers.
- Laser fault injection to manipulate memory contents.

Impact: Can lead to system crashes, data corruption, and security breaches.

2. Software Attack Vectors:

Malware and Viruses:

Malicious software designed to infiltrate and damage CPS components.

Examples:

- Ransomware that encrypts critical data and disrupts operations.
- Viruses that propagate through networks and infect control systems.
- Stuxnet: a famous worm that targeted industrial control systems.

Impact: Can lead to data loss, system disruption, and physical damage.

Software Vulnerabilities:

Exploiting flaws in software code, such as buffer overflows, injection attacks, and logic errors.

Examples:

- Exploiting vulnerabilities in RTOS (Real-Time Operating Systems) to gain control of critical processes.
- Injecting malicious code into web interfaces used to control CPS.

Impact: Can lead to unauthorized access, data manipulation, and system crashes.

Firmware Attacks:

Targeting the firmware that controls hardware components.

Examples:

- Replacing legitimate firmware with malicious firmware to manipulate device behavior.
- Exploiting vulnerabilities in firmware update mechanisms.

Impact: Can lead to hardware manipulation, data breaches, and system disruption.

3. Network Attack Vectors:

Network Intrusion:

Gaining unauthorized access to CPS networks through vulnerabilities in network devices or protocols.

Examples:

- Exploiting vulnerabilities in firewalls or routers.
- Using phishing attacks to obtain network credentials.

Impact: Can lead to data breaches, system disruption, and control system manipulation.

Denial-of-Service (DoS) Attacks:

Overwhelming CPS networks with traffic to disrupt communication and control.

Examples:

- Flooding control systems with network requests.
- Disrupting communication between sensors and actuators.

Impact: Can lead to system shutdown, process disruption, and safety hazards.

Man-in-the-Middle Attacks:

Intercepting and manipulating communication between CPS components.

Examples:

- Intercepting and modifying sensor data.
- Manipulating control commands sent to actuators.

Impact: Can lead to data manipulation, process disruption, and safety hazards.

Data Injection Attacks:

Inserting false data into sensor streams or control signals.

Examples:

- Sending false sensor data to a control system to cause it to make incorrect decisions.
- Injecting malicious commands into a network to control actuators.

Impact: Can lead to process disruption, physical damage, and safety hazards.

Understanding these attack vectors is crucial for developing effective security measures to protect CPS from cyber threats. A layered security approach, combining hardware, software, and network security measures, is essential for mitigating the risks associated with these complex systems.

COMMON SECURITY THREATS: MALWARE, DENIAL-OF-SERVICE, AND DATA BREACHES

In the contemporary digital landscape, organizations face a barrage of security threats, with malware, Denial-of-Service (DoS) attacks, and data breaches being among the most prevalent and damaging. These threats exploit vulnerabilities in systems and human behavior, leading to significant financial losses, reputational damage, and operational disruptions. Malware, short for malicious software, encompasses a wide range of harmful programs designed to infiltrate and damage computer systems. This includes viruses, worms, Trojans, ransomware, and spyware. Viruses replicate by attaching themselves to legitimate files, while worms propagate independently across networks. Trojans disguise themselves as legitimate software to trick users into installing them. Ransomware encrypts files and demands payment for decryption, and spyware secretly monitors user activity. Each type of malware employs different techniques to achieve its objectives, but all share the common goal of compromising system integrity and confidentiality.

Denial-of-Service (DoS) attacks aim to disrupt the availability of online services by overwhelming them with traffic. This can be achieved through various methods, such as flooding servers with requests, exploiting vulnerabilities in network protocols, or launching distributed attacks from multiple compromised devices (DDoS). The impact of DoS attacks can range from temporary service outages to prolonged disruptions, causing significant financial losses and customer dissatisfaction. These attacks are particularly challenging to defend against due to their distributed nature and the difficulty of distinguishing legitimate traffic from malicious requests.

Data breaches, on the other hand, involve the unauthorized access or disclosure of sensitive information. These breaches can be caused by a variety of factors, including malware infections, phishing attacks, insider threats, and human errors. The consequences of data breaches can be severe, including financial losses from regulatory fines and legal settlements, reputational damage from loss of customer trust, and operational disruptions from system downtime. The increasing volume and sensitivity of data being collected and stored by organizations make data breaches a growing concern.

The interconnectedness of modern systems amplifies the impact of these threats. Malware can spread rapidly across networks, infecting multiple devices and disrupting critical operations. DoS attacks can target essential services, causing widespread outages and impacting numerous users. Data breaches can expose sensitive information, leading to identity theft, financial fraud, and other malicious activities. To mitigate these threats, organizations must adopt a multi-layered security approach. This includes implementing robust endpoint protection to detect and prevent malware infections, deploying intrusion detection and prevention systems to identify and block malicious network traffic, and enforcing strong access controls to protect sensitive data. Regular security assessments and penetration testing can help identify and address vulnerabilities before they can be exploited by attackers.

Employee training and awareness programs are also essential for preventing security incidents. Many successful attacks rely on social engineering techniques, such as phishing, which trick users into revealing sensitive information or clicking on malicious links.

By educating employees about security best practices and raising awareness of common threats, organizations can reduce the risk of human error. Incident response planning is another crucial aspect of cybersecurity. Organizations should have well-defined procedures for responding to security incidents, including steps for containing the damage, recovering from the attack, and restoring normal operations. This includes having robust backup and recovery strategies in place to minimize the impact of data breaches and ransomware attacks. Continuous monitoring and threat intelligence are also essential for detecting and responding to security incidents in real-time. By staying informed about the latest threats and vulnerabilities, organizations can proactively adapt their security measures to stay ahead of attackers.

VULNERABILITIES IN INDUSTRIAL CONTROL SYSTEMS (ICS)

Industrial Control Systems (ICS), which manage and control critical infrastructure and industrial processes, face unique and complex cybersecurity challenges. Unlike traditional IT systems, ICS are often designed for long lifespans, operate in real-time, and interact directly with the physical world. These characteristics make them particularly vulnerable to cyberattacks, which can have devastating consequences for safety, reliability, and productivity. One of the primary vulnerabilities in ICS is the use of legacy hardware and software. Many ICS components are outdated and lack modern security features, making them susceptible to known vulnerabilities. Patching and updating these systems can be challenging due to their critical nature and the need to minimize downtime. The long lifespans of ICS also mean that they may not have been designed with security in mind, as cybersecurity was not a primary concern when they were initially deployed.

Another significant vulnerability is the lack of network segmentation. In many ICS environments, there is a lack of clear separation between the operational technology (OT) network and the IT network. This allows attackers to move laterally between networks, gaining access to critical control systems from compromised IT devices. The use of proprietary protocols and communication standards in ICS also poses a challenge. These protocols are often poorly documented and lack robust security features, making them vulnerable to reverse engineering and exploitation. The increasing connectivity of ICS to the internet and other external networks further expands the attack surface. This allows attackers to remotely access control systems and launch attacks from anywhere in the world.

Human error is another significant vulnerability in ICS environments. Operators and engineers may inadvertently introduce security risks through misconfigurations, unauthorized software installations, or the use of weak passwords. Social engineering attacks, such as phishing, can also trick employees into revealing sensitive information or clicking on malicious links.

The consequences of cyberattacks on ICS can be severe. Attacks can disrupt critical infrastructure, such as power grids, water treatment plants, and transportation systems, leading to widespread outages and safety hazards. They can also disrupt industrial processes, causing production delays, financial losses, and environmental damage. The Stuxnet worm, which targeted Iranian nuclear facilities, is a prime example of the potential impact of cyberattacks on ICS.

To mitigate vulnerabilities in ICS, organizations must adopt a defense-in-depth approach. This involves implementing multiple layers of security controls, including network segmentation, intrusion detection and prevention systems, and robust access controls. Regular security assessments and vulnerability scanning can help identify and address weaknesses in ICS environments. Patch management is also crucial for keeping systems up to date with the latest security patches. However, patching ICS can be challenging due to the need to minimize downtime and the potential for compatibility issues. Organizations should establish a risk-based approach to patching, prioritizing critical systems and conducting thorough testing before deploying patches.

Secure remote access is another essential aspect of ICS security. Organizations should implement strong authentication and authorization mechanisms for remote access, and use virtual private networks (VPNs) to encrypt communication. Incident response planning is also crucial for ICS environments. Organizations should have well-defined procedures for responding to cyberattacks, including steps for isolating compromised systems, restoring backups, and communicating with stakeholders. Employee training and awareness programs are essential for preventing human error and social engineering attacks. By educating employees about ICS security best practices, organizations can reduce the risk of insider threats and inadvertent security breaches.

RISK ASSESSMENT AND MANAGEMENT

Risk assessment and management are fundamental components of a robust cybersecurity strategy. In an increasingly interconnected and threat-laden digital world, organizations must proactively identify, evaluate, and mitigate potential risks to protect their assets, data, and operations. Risk assessment involves the process of identifying and analyzing potential threats and vulnerabilities that could impact an organization. This includes assessing the likelihood and impact of various risks, such as cyberattacks, natural disasters, and human errors. The goal is to gain a comprehensive understanding of the organization's risk landscape and prioritize mitigation efforts.

A well-conducted risk assessment should consider all aspects of the organization, including its physical infrastructure, IT systems, data, and personnel. This involves identifying critical assets, assessing potential threats and vulnerabilities, and evaluating the potential impact of security incidents. Various risk assessment methodologies and frameworks exist, such as NIST's Risk Management Framework (RMF), ISO 27005, and FAIR (Factor Analysis of Information Risk). These frameworks provide a structured approach to risk assessment, ensuring that all relevant factors are considered.

Risk management, on the other hand, involves the process of developing and implementing strategies to mitigate identified risks. This includes selecting and implementing appropriate security controls, developing incident response plans, and establishing policies and procedures for managing risk. Risk management is an ongoing process that requires continuous monitoring and evaluation to ensure that security controls remain effective and that new risks are addressed.

Effective risk management involves several key steps. First, organizations must establish a risk management framework that defines the roles and responsibilities of personnel involved in risk management. This includes establishing a risk management committee and assigning responsibility for specific risk areas. Second, organizations must develop a risk assessment methodology that defines the criteria for evaluating risks. This includes defining the likelihood and impact of various risks, as well

SECURITY MECHANISMS AND PROTOCOLS

In the digital realm, where data is both the lifeblood and the target, robust security mechanisms and protocols are indispensable for safeguarding sensitive information and maintaining trust. These safeguards, ranging from encryption and authentication to access control and secure communication protocols, form the foundation of a resilient cybersecurity posture. [2] As the threat landscape evolves with increasing sophistication, understanding and implementing effective security measures becomes paramount. This section will explore the essential security mechanisms and protocols that organizations employ to protect their systems and data, highlighting their importance in mitigating risks and ensuring the integrity and confidentiality of digital assets.

AUTHENTICATION AND ACCESS CONTROL

Authentication and Access Control are fundamental pillars of secure user management. They work in tandem to ensure that only authorized individuals can access sensitive systems and data, and that they can only perform actions they are permitted to do. Let's break down each component and their relationship:

1. Authentication:

Authentication is the process of verifying a user's identity.

Methods:

Password-based authentication: This is the most common method, requiring users to enter a username and password. However, it's also vulnerable to attacks like password guessing, phishing, and brute-force attacks.

Multi-factor authentication (MFA): MFA adds layers of security by requiring users to provide multiple forms of identification. Common factors include:

- **Something you know:** (password, PIN)
- **Something you have:** (smartphone, security token, smart card)
- **Something you are:** (biometrics, such as fingerprint or facial recognition)

- Biometric authentication: Uses unique biological traits to verify identity.
- Certificate-based authentication: Uses digital certificates to verify the identity of users and devices.
- Token-based authentication: Uses security tokens, such as JSON Web Tokens (JWTs), to verify user identity.
- Single Sign-On (SSO): Allows users to log in once and access multiple applications without re-entering their credentials.

2. Access Control:

Access control determines what actions an authenticated user is allowed to perform. It answers the question, "What are you allowed to do?"

Models:

- **Role-Based Access Control (RBAC):** Assigns permissions to roles, and then assigns users to those roles. This simplifies management and ensures consistency.

- **Attribute-Based Access Control (ABAC):** Grants or denies access based on attributes of the user, resource, and environment. This provides fine-grained control and flexibility.
- **Discretionary Access Control (DAC):** Allows resource owners to control who has access to their resources.
- **Mandatory Access Control (MAC):** Uses security labels to enforce access restrictions. This is often used in high-security environments.

Implementation:

- Users should only have the minimum necessary permissions to perform their job functions.
- Dividing critical tasks among multiple users to prevent fraud and errors.
- Tracking access attempts and actions to detect and investigate security incidents.

Relationship between Authentication and Access Control:

- Authentication must occur before access control. Without verifying a user's identity, it's impossible to determine their authorized actions.
- Authentication establishes the "who," and access control establishes the "what." They are interdependent.
- Effective access control relies on strong authentication. Weak authentication can compromise the entire access control system.
- Together, they form a security perimeter. Authentication verifies the person requesting access, and access control defines the parameters of allowed usage.

Why are they Important?

- Prevents unauthorized access to sensitive information.
- Protects critical systems from malicious activity.
- Helps organizations meet regulatory requirements.
- Enables tracking of user actions for auditing and investigation.
- Minimizes the risk of disruptions caused by security breaches.
- A secure system builds user trust.

In essence, robust Authentication and Access Control mechanisms are vital for protecting digital assets and maintaining a secure computing environment.

ENCRYPTION AND DATA PROTECTION: PROTECTING SENSITIVE INFORMATION

The Fundamentals of Encryption

Encryption is the process of converting plaintext (readable data) into ciphertext (unreadable data) using an algorithm (cipher) and a key. This ensures that even if unauthorized individuals gain access to the encrypted data, they cannot understand it without the decryption key.

Why Encrypt?

- Protects sensitive information from unauthorized access.
- Ensures data has not been tampered with.
- Can be used to verify the sender of a message.
- Many regulations require encryption of sensitive data.

Types of Encryption:

- **Symmetric-key encryption:** Uses the same key for both encryption and decryption. It's fast and efficient but requires secure key distribution. Examples: AES, DES.
- **Asymmetric-key encryption (Public-key cryptography):** Uses a pair of keys: a public key for encryption and a private key for decryption. The public key can be shared, but the private key must be kept secret. Examples: RSA, ECC.

- **Hashing:** A one-way function that creates a fixed-size "fingerprint" of data. It's used to verify data integrity but cannot be used to recover the original data. Examples: SHA-256, MD5.

Encryption in Practice:

- Encrypting data stored on hard drives, databases, and other storage devices.
- Encrypting data transmitted over networks, such as the internet. Examples: TLS/SSL for web traffic, VPNs for secure remote access.
- Encrypting data on the sender's device and decrypting it only on the recipient's device, ensuring that no one in between can read it.

Data Protection Strategies and Implementation

Beyond encryption, comprehensive data protection involves a multi-layered approach.

- **Data Loss Prevention (DLP):**

  - DLP systems monitor and control the movement of sensitive data to prevent it from leaving the organization's control.
  - They can identify and block unauthorized data transfers, such as emails, file transfers, and USB drives.
  - DLP helps enforce data security policies and comply with regulations.

- **Key Management:**

  - Securely generating, storing, distributing, and destroying encryption keys is crucial.
  - Key management systems (KMS) automate key management tasks and provide centralized control.

- Proper key rotation is essential to minimize the impact of compromised keys.

- **Access Control and Data Minimization:**

  - Restrict access to sensitive data to authorized users only.
  - Implement the principle of least privilege.
  - Collect and store only the data that is necessary.
  - Regularly review and revoke access permissions.

- **Data Backup and Recovery:**

  - Regularly back up critical data to ensure it can be recovered in case of data loss or disaster.
  - Store backups in a secure and off-site location.
  - Test backup and recovery procedures regularly.

- **Data Masking and Tokenization:**

  - Data masking replaces sensitive data with realistic but fake data for testing and development purposes.
  - Tokenization replaces sensitive data with non-sensitive tokens, which can be used to access the original data through a secure vault.
  - These techniques help protect sensitive data while still allowing it to be used for legitimate purposes.

- **Regulatory Compliance:**

  - Organizations must comply with various data protection regulations, such as GDPR, HIPAA, and CCPA.
  - These regulations often require specific encryption and data protection measures.

INTRUSION DETECTION AND PREVENTION SYSTEMS

Understanding IDPS Functionality

Intrusion Detection and Prevention Systems (IDPS) are security tools that monitor network traffic and system activity for malicious behavior. IDPS can detect and prevent attacks in real-time.

Intrusion Detection Systems (IDS): IDS passively monitor network traffic and system logs for suspicious activity. They generate alerts when an intrusion is detected. IDS primarily focus on detection and reporting.

Intrusion Prevention Systems (IPS): IPS actively block or prevent malicious traffic and activity. They can drop malicious packets, terminate connections, and block IP addresses. IPS provide real-time protection.

Types of IDPS:

- **Network-based IDPS (NIDS):** Monitors network traffic for malicious activity.
- **Host-based IDPS (HIDS):** Monitors system activity on individual hosts.
- **Signature-based IDPS:** Detects known attacks by matching network traffic or system activity against a database of signatures.
- **Anomaly-based IDPS:** Detects unknown attacks by identifying deviations from normal behavior.
- **Hybrid IDPS:** Combines signature-based and anomaly-based detection.

Key IDPS Components:

- Collect network traffic and system activity data.
- Analyze the collected data for malicious activity.
- Provides a centralized interface for configuring and managing the IDPS.
- Stores signatures, rules, and event logs.

IDPS Implementation and Best Practices

Effective IDPS deployment requires careful planning and implementation.

Deployment Strategies: Place NIDS sensors at strategic points in the network, such as the perimeter and critical network segments. Deploy HIDS agents on critical servers and workstations. Choose the appropriate IDPS type based on the organization's needs and risk profile.

Signature and Rule Management: Keep signature databases and rules up to date. Customize rules to match the organization's specific environment. Regularly test and tune rules to minimize false positives and false negatives.

Alert Management: Develop a process for responding to IDPS alerts. Prioritize alerts based on severity. Investigate and document all security incidents.

FIREWALLS AND NETWORK SECURITY

The Role of Firewalls

Firewalls are network security devices that monitor and control network traffic based on predefined security rules. They act as a barrier between a trusted internal network and an untrusted external network, such as the internet.

Firewall Functions:

- **Packet filtering:** Inspecting network packets and allowing or blocking them based on source and destination IP addresses, ports, and protocols.
- **Stateful inspection:** Tracking the state of network connections and allowing or blocking packets based on the connection state.
- **Application-layer filtering:** Inspecting the contents of network packets at the application layer and blocking malicious traffic based on application-specific rules.
- **Network Address Translation (NAT):** Translating private IP addresses to public IP addresses, allowing multiple devices on a private network to share a single public IP address.

- ○ **Virtual Private Network (VPN):** Creating secure connections between remote users and the internal network.

Types of Firewalls:

- ○ **Packet-filtering firewalls:** The most basic type, filtering packets based on IP addresses, ports, and protocols.
- ○ **Stateful firewalls:** Track the state of connections and provide more advanced filtering.
- ○ **Next-generation firewalls (NGFWs):** Combine traditional firewall functions with advanced features, such as intrusion prevention, application control, and deep packet inspection.
- ○ **Hardware firewalls:** Dedicated hardware devices that provide high performance and security.
- ○ **Software firewalls:** Software applications that run on individual computers or servers.

Network Security Best Practices

Firewalls are a critical component of network security, but they must be implemented as part of a comprehensive security strategy.

Perimeter Security:

- ○ Deploy firewalls at the network perimeter to protect the internal network from external threats.
- ○ Use demilitarized zones (DMZs) to isolate public-facing servers from the internal network.

Internal Network Segmentation:

- ○ Segment the internal network into different security zones based on

RESILIENCE AND FAULT TOLERANCE

In the relentless march of technological advancement, our reliance on complex systems has grown exponentially. From critical infrastructure to everyday applications, the expectation of uninterrupted service has become a fundamental demand. However, the reality of computing is that failures are inevitable. Hardware malfunctions, software bugs, network outages, and even human error can disrupt operations, leading to costly downtime and data loss. This is where the principles of resilience and fault tolerance become indispensable. They represent a paradigm shift from simply preventing failures to building systems that can gracefully handle them, ensuring continuity and minimizing impact.

Resilience, at its core, is the ability of a system to adapt and recover from disruptions, returning to its normal operating state as quickly as possible. It encompasses the strategies and mechanisms that enable a system to absorb shocks and bounce back. Fault tolerance, a closely related concept, focuses on designing systems that can continue to operate correctly even when individual components fail. This is achieved through redundancy, error detection, and recovery mechanisms that allow the system to mask failures and maintain functionality.

The importance of resilience and fault tolerance cannot be overstated. In critical sectors like healthcare, finance, and transportation, system failures can have catastrophic consequences. For businesses, downtime translates to lost revenue, damaged reputation, and customer dissatisfaction. Even in everyday applications, users expect seamless and reliable experiences. Implementing these principles requires a holistic approach, encompassing hardware, software, and operational procedures.

One key aspect of building resilient systems is redundancy. By duplicating critical components, such as servers, storage devices, and network connections, the system can continue operating even if one component fails. Load balancing, a technique for distributing workloads across multiple resources, further enhances resilience by preventing any single point of failure from overloading the system. Error detection and correction mechanisms, such as checksums and parity bits, help identify and mitigate data corruption.

Software plays a crucial role in enabling fault tolerance. Techniques like transaction management, which ensures that database operations are atomic and consistent, prevent data inconsistencies in the event of failures. Checkpointing, a method for periodically saving the state of a system, allows for quick recovery in case of crashes. Microservices architectures, which break down applications into smaller, independent services, enhance resilience by isolating failures and enabling independent scaling.

Beyond technical implementations, operational procedures are essential for maintaining resilience. Monitoring and alerting systems provide real-time visibility into system health, allowing for proactive intervention. Incident response plans outline the steps to be taken in the event of a failure, ensuring a coordinated and efficient recovery. Regular testing and simulations, such as chaos engineering, help identify weaknesses and improve the system's ability to withstand disruptions.

In conclusion, resilience and fault tolerance are not merely buzzwords but fundamental principles for building robust and dependable systems. By embracing these concepts, organizations can minimize the impact of failures, ensure business continuity, and deliver reliable services to their users. In an increasingly interconnected and demanding digital world, building systems that endure is no longer a luxury but a necessity.

1. DESIGNING FOR RESILIENCE: REDUNDANCY AND DIVERSITY

The Foundation of Redundancy

Redundancy is the cornerstone of designing systems that can withstand failures. It involves duplicating critical components or functionalities to ensure that if one part fails, another can take over seamlessly. This principle is not about eliminating failures, which are often inevitable, but about mitigating their impact and maintaining operational continuity.

Types of Redundancy:

- **Hardware Redundancy:** Duplicating physical components like servers, storage devices, power supplies, and network connections. Examples include RAID (Redundant Array of Independent Disks) for storage, redundant power supplies in servers, and multiple network paths.
- **Software Redundancy:** Implementing backup software systems or processes. This includes redundant code modules, backup databases, and failover mechanisms.
- **Data Redundancy:** Creating multiple copies of critical data in different locations or storage systems. This ensures data availability in case of hardware failures, data corruption, or disasters.
- **Geographic Redundancy:** Distributing system components across multiple geographically diverse locations. This protects against regional disasters like earthquakes, floods, or power outages.
- **Time Redundancy:** Performing critical operations multiple times to detect and correct transient errors.

Benefits of Redundancy:

- **Increased Availability:** Minimizes downtime by providing backup components.
- **Improved Fault Tolerance:** Enables the system to continue operating despite component failures.
- **Enhanced Reliability:** Reduces the likelihood of system-wide failures.
- **Disaster Recovery:** Facilitates quick recovery from catastrophic events.

The Power of Diversity

While redundancy focuses on duplication, diversity aims to mitigate common-mode failures, where multiple components fail simultaneously due to a shared vulnerability. By introducing diversity, we create systems that are less susceptible to single points of failure.

Types of Diversity:

- **Hardware Diversity:** Using different hardware architectures or manufacturers for critical components.
- **Software Diversity:** Employing different operating systems, programming languages, or software libraries.
- **Data Diversity:** Storing data in different formats or databases.
- **Environmental Diversity:** Deploying systems in different physical environments to reduce the impact of environmental factors.
- **Algorithm Diversity:** Using diverse algorithms to perform the same function.

Benefits of Diversity:

- **Reduced Common-Mode Failures:** Prevents simultaneous failures due to shared vulnerabilities.
- **Increased System Robustness:** Makes the system more resilient to unforeseen errors or attacks.
- **Enhanced Security:** Limits the impact of vulnerabilities that affect specific hardware or software.
- **Improved Adaptability:** Enables the system to adapt to changing conditions or requirements.

Balancing Redundancy and Diversity:

- Redundancy and diversity are complementary strategies.
- The optimal balance depends on the specific system requirements and risk tolerance.
- Overly redundant systems can be complex and expensive.
- Excessive diversity can increase complexity and maintenance overhead.

- A well-designed system should incorporate both redundancy and diversity to achieve optimal resilience.

FAULT DETECTION AND RECOVERY MECHANISMS (2 PAGES)

The Importance of Fault Detection

Fault detection is the process of identifying errors or failures within a system. Early detection is crucial for minimizing the impact of faults and preventing them from cascading into larger failures. Effective fault detection mechanisms are essential for building resilient systems.

Types of Fault Detection:

- **Hardware Fault Detection:** Monitoring hardware components for errors, such as voltage fluctuations, temperature anomalies, or communication failures.
- **Software Fault Detection:** Detecting errors in software code, such as runtime exceptions, memory leaks, or logical errors.
- **Data Fault Detection:** Verifying the integrity and consistency of data, such as checksums, parity bits, or data validation rules.
- **Network Fault Detection:** Monitoring network traffic for errors, such as packet loss, network congestion, or connection failures.
- **Anomaly Detection:** Identifying deviations from normal system behavior, which may indicate a fault or attack.

Fault Detection Techniques:

- **Monitoring and Alerting:** Continuously monitoring system parameters and generating alerts when anomalies are detected.
- **Self-Testing:** Implementing built-in tests that automatically check the functionality of system components.

- ◦ **Error Codes and Logging:** Generating error codes and logging events to track faults and diagnose problems.
- ◦ **Watchdog Timers:** Using timers to detect system hangs or unresponsive processes.
- ◦ **Redundancy Checks:** Comparing the outputs of redundant components to detect inconsistencies.

Implementing Effective Recovery Mechanisms

Once a fault is detected, recovery mechanisms are needed to restore the system to a functional state. Recovery mechanisms aim to minimize downtime and data loss.

Types of Recovery Mechanisms:

- ◦ **Automatic Recovery:** Automatically restoring the system to a previous state or switching to a backup component.
- ◦ **Manual Recovery:** Requiring human intervention to diagnose and resolve the fault.
- ◦ **Rollback:** Reverting the system to a previous known good state.
- ◦ **Failover:** Switching to a redundant component or system.
- ◦ **Graceful Degradation:** Reducing the system's functionality in a controlled manner to maintain essential services.
- ◦ **Error Correction:** Correcting data errors using techniques like forward error correction or retransmission. .

CYBER-PHYSICAL RESILIENCE: ADAPTING TO ATTACKS AND FAILURES

The Convergence of Cyber and Physical Systems

Cyber-Physical Systems (CPS) integrate computing, networking, and physical processes. These systems are increasingly prevalent in critical infrastructure, such as power grids, transportation systems, and industrial control systems. The convergence of cyber and physical domains introduces new challenges for resilience, as attacks and failures can have physical consequences.

Characteristics of Cyber-Physical Systems:

- **Real-Time Interaction:** CPS interact with the physical world in real-time.
- **Feedback Loops:** CPS use sensors and actuators to control physical processes.
- **Interconnectivity:** CPS are often interconnected with other systems and networks.
- **Critical Infrastructure:** CPS are often used in critical infrastructure applications.

- **Cyber-Physical Security Threats:**

  - **Physical Attacks:** Attacks that target the physical components of CPS, such as tampering with sensors or actuators.
  - **Cyber Attacks:** Attacks that target the cyber components of CPS, such as malware infections, denial-of-service attacks, or data breaches.
  - **Combined Attacks:** Attacks that combine cyber and physical elements, such as using malware to manipulate physical processes.
  - **Cascading Failures:** Failures that propagate from one component to another, leading to widespread disruptions.

Building Cyber-Physical Resilience

Building resilient CPS requires a holistic approach that addresses both cyber and physical threats.

Key Strategies for Cyber-Physical Resilience:

- Secure Design: Designing CPS with security in mind from the ground up.
- Intrusion Detection and Prevention: Implementing systems to detect and prevent cyber attacks.
- Physical Security: Protecting physical components from tampering and unauthorized access.

- Redundancy and Diversity: Incorporating redundancy and diversity into both cyber and physical components.
- Fault Tolerance: Designing CPS to continue operating despite failures or attacks.
- Resilient Control Systems: Implementing control systems that can adapt to changing conditions and mitigate the impact of attacks.
- Situational Awareness: Monitoring the state of the system and the environment to detect anomalies and threats.
- Incident Response and Recovery: Developing plans for responding to security incidents and system failures.
- Collaboration and Information Sharing: Sharing threat intelligence and best practices with other organizations.

Challenges of Cyber-Physical Resilience:

- CPS are often highly complex, making it difficult to identify and mitigate all potential threats.
- CPS are often interconnected with other systems, creating complex dependencies that can be difficult to manage.
- Many CPS are based on legacy systems that may not have been designed with security in mind.
- CPS often have real-time constraints, making it challenging to implement security measures that do not introduce latency.

FIVE

PRACTICAL IMPLEMENTATION AND CASE STUDIES

Transitioning from theoretical concepts to tangible applications, the realm of practical implementation and case studies provides invaluable insights into the real-world efficacy of cybersecurity principles.

This section delves into the critical process of translating security frameworks and methodologies into operational realities, examining how organizations navigate the complexities of safeguarding their digital assets. By scrutinizing real-world scenarios, we gain a deeper understanding of the challenges encountered, the strategies employed, and the lessons learned in the pursuit of robust cybersecurity. Through detailed case studies, we will explore the nuanced application of security measures across diverse industries, highlighting both successes and failures. This practical exploration will demonstrate how abstract security concepts, like resilience, encryption, and intrusion detection, are deployed, adapted, and refined to address the ever-evolving threat landscape. Furthermore, we will analyze the impact of these implementations on organizational operations, compliance, and overall security posture, providing a comprehensive view of the practical dimensions of cybersecurity.

DEVELOPMENT TOOLS AND PLATFORMS

The landscape of software development has undergone a dramatic transformation, driven by the need for rapid innovation, scalability, and security. At the heart of this evolution lie development tools and platforms, which have become indispensable for building, deploying, and maintaining modern applications. This section will delve into the critical role these tools play in streamlining the development lifecycle, enhancing collaboration, and fortifying security postures. We'll explore how platforms like cloud-based development environments, containerization technologies, and automated security testing tools are revolutionizing the way applications are created and managed. Through a detailed examination of these technologies, we aim to provide a comprehensive understanding of how developers leverage them to build secure, efficient, and resilient software. Moreover, we will address the challenges and best practices associated with integrating these tools into existing workflows, ensuring that organizations can effectively harness their potential to drive innovation while mitigating security risks.

1. PROGRAMMING LANGUAGES AND FRAMEWORKS: PYTHON, C++, ROS (2 PAGES)

The Versatility of Python and C++

Programming languages are the bedrock of software development, and in the realm of CPS, Python and C++ stand out for their distinct strengths. Python, with its readability and extensive libraries, excels in rapid prototyping and data processing. Its ease of use makes it ideal for integrating diverse components and implementing high-level control algorithms. Libraries like NumPy, SciPy, and TensorFlow provide powerful tools for numerical computation, signal processing, and machine learning, all crucial for intelligent CPS. C++, on the other hand, offers unparalleled performance and low-level control, making it essential for real-time systems and resource-constrained environments. Its ability to directly manipulate hardware and optimize code for speed is critical for applications where latency and efficiency are paramount, such as embedded systems and robotics. The combination of these two languages allows developers to build systems that are both agile and robust, leveraging Python for high-level logic and C++ for critical performance-sensitive tasks.

ROS: The Robotics Operating System

The Robot Operating System (ROS) is a flexible framework for writing robot software. It's not an operating system in the traditional sense, but rather a collection of tools, libraries, and conventions that simplify the development of complex robotic systems. ROS provides a modular architecture that allows developers to create reusable components, known as nodes, which communicate with each other through a message-passing system. This architecture facilitates collaboration and code reuse, accelerating the development process. ROS also provides a rich set of tools for visualization, simulation, and debugging, enabling developers to test and validate their code in a virtual environment before deploying it to physical robots. ROS's open-source nature and large community contribute to its continuous development and expansion, making it a powerful platform for building a wide range of robotic applications, from autonomous vehicles to industrial robots. ROS 2, the next generation of ROS, further enhances its capabilities by introducing real-time support, improved security, and better support for distributed systems, addressing the evolving needs of modern CPS. Furthermore, the combination of ROS with python and C++ allows developers to build systems that have both high performance critical components, and high level logic.

2. SIMULATION AND MODELING TOOLS: MATLAB/SIMULINK, GAZEBO

MATLAB/Simulink: Modeling and Simulation Powerhouse

MATLAB/Simulink is a powerful suite of tools for modeling, simulating, and analyzing dynamic systems. Its graphical environment allows engineers to create block diagrams that represent complex systems, making it easier to visualize and understand their behavior. Simulink's ability to simulate continuous-time and discrete-time systems makes it ideal for modeling a wide range of CPS, from control systems and signal processing to communication networks and power systems. MATLAB's extensive libraries provide a rich set of functions for numerical computation, data analysis, and visualization, enabling engineers to perform in-depth analysis of simulation results. The ability to generate C/C++ code from Simulink models facilitates the deployment of control algorithms to embedded systems, bridging the gap between simulation and implementation. MATLAB/Simulink's comprehensive toolset and intuitive interface make it an indispensable tool for designing and validating CPS before deployment, reducing development time and cost.

Gazebo: Realistic Robotics Simulation

Gazebo is a powerful 3D robotics simulator that allows developers to test and validate their robot software in a realistic virtual environment. Gazebo simulates the physics of the real world, including collisions, friction, and gravity, providing a high-fidelity simulation of robot behavior. Gazebo's ability to simulate a wide range of sensors, such as cameras, lidar, and IMUs, enables developers to test their robot software with realistic sensor data. Gazebo's open-source nature and modular architecture make it highly extensible, allowing developers to customize the simulation environment to meet their specific needs. Gazebo's integration with ROS further enhances its capabilities, enabling developers to seamlessly transition from simulation to real-world deployment. Gazebo's ability to simulate complex environments and robot behaviors makes it an invaluable tool for developing and testing autonomous robots, reducing the risk of damage to hardware and the environment. Gazebo's ability to simulate a wide range of environments and sensors makes it a key tool for testing AI algorithms in an environment that mimics the real world.

3. CLOUD PLATFORMS FOR CPS: AWS IOT, AZURE IOT, GOOGLE CLOUD IOT

AWS IoT: Scalable and Secure IoT Solutions

Amazon Web Services (AWS) IoT provides a comprehensive suite of services for connecting, managing, and securing IoT devices. AWS IoT Core allows devices to securely connect to the cloud and exchange data using MQTT, HTTP, and other protocols. AWS IoT Device Management provides tools for onboarding, organizing, monitoring, and remotely managing devices at scale. AWS IoT Analytics enables developers to analyze IoT data and gain insights into device behavior. AWS IoT Greengrass extends AWS capabilities to edge devices, allowing them to perform local processing and decision-making even when disconnected from the cloud. AWS IoT's scalability, security, and comprehensive feature set make it a powerful platform for building a wide range of IoT applications, from smart homes and industrial automation to connected vehicles and healthcare. AWS IoT allows for easy integration with other AWS services such as Lambda, S3, and DynamoDB. This allows for powerful data processing and storage pipelines.

Azure IoT and Google Cloud IoT: Connecting and Managing Devices

Microsoft Azure IoT provides a similar set of services for connecting, managing, and securing IoT devices. Azure IoT Hub acts as a central message hub for bidirectional communication between devices and the cloud. Azure IoT Device Provisioning Service simplifies the process of onboarding and provisioning devices at scale. Azure IoT Edge enables edge devices to perform local processing and analytics. Azure IoT Central provides a platform for building and managing IoT solutions without writing code. Azure IoT's integration with other Azure services, such as Azure Stream Analytics and Azure Machine Learning, enables developers to build powerful IoT applications. Google Cloud IoT Core provides a managed service for connecting, managing, and ingesting data from globally distributed devices. Google Cloud IoT Edge extends cloud intelligence to edge devices, enabling local processing and decision-making. Google Cloud IoT's integration with other Google Cloud services, such as BigQuery and Cloud Machine Learning Engine, enables developers to build powerful data analytics and machine learning applications for IoT. All three cloud platforms offer robust security features, including device authentication, authorization, and data encryption, ensuring the security of IoT deployments. The ability to use each cloud platforms machine learning capabilities allows for the creation of intelligent cyber physical systems.

4. OPEN SOURCE TOOLS AND LIBRARIES (2 PAGES)

The Power of Open Source in CPS Development

Open-source tools and libraries play a crucial role in the development of CPS, offering a wealth of resources and fostering collaboration among developers. These tools provide access to cutting-edge technologies and algorithms without the need for expensive commercial licenses, making them particularly valuable for research and development. Open-source libraries like OpenCV provide powerful tools for computer vision, enabling developers to build applications that can analyze and interpret visual data. Libraries like TensorFlow and PyTorch provide frameworks for machine learning, enabling developers to build intelligent systems that can learn and adapt to their environment. Open-source operating systems like Linux provide a stable and flexible platform for running CPS software, offering a wide range of device drivers and networking capabilities. Open-source middleware like MQTT and DDS provide communication protocols for connecting and exchanging data between devices, enabling the development of distributed CPS.

Leveraging Open Source for Innovation and Collaboration

The open-source community provides a vibrant ecosystem for sharing knowledge and collaborating on projects. Open-source projects often have active communities that provide support and contribute to the development of new features and bug fixes. Open-source tools and libraries are often highly customizable, allowing developers to adapt them to their specific needs. Open-source projects foster innovation by encouraging the sharing of ideas and code, leading to the development of new technologies and applications. Open-source tools and libraries are often well-documented, making them easier to learn and use. Open-source software promotes transparency and security, as the source code is publicly available for review and auditing. The ability to use open source tools across multiple platforms, and hardware types, increases the speed of cyber physical system development.

CASESTUDIES

SMART GRID AUTOMATION AND SECURITY

Overview of Smart Grid Technologies and Intelligent Monitoring/Control

The smart grid represents a modernization of the traditional electrical grid, integrating digital technologies to enhance efficiency, reliability, and sustainability. At its core, smart grids utilize advanced sensing, communication, and control systems to enable real-time monitoring and management of electricity flow. Smart meters, deployed at consumer premises, provide granular data on energy consumption, enabling dynamic pricing and demand response programs. Phasor Measurement Units (PMUs) offer high-resolution measurements of voltage and current, enabling precise monitoring of grid stability. Distributed Energy Resources (DERs), such as solar panels and wind turbines, are integrated into the grid, allowing for decentralized power generation and consumption. Intelligent monitoring and control systems leverage this data to optimize grid operations. Advanced Distribution Management Systems (ADMS) automate fault detection, isolation, and restoration, minimizing outages and improving grid resilience. Energy Management Systems (EMS) optimize power generation and distribution, balancing supply and demand in real-time. These technologies enable a more flexible and responsive grid, capable of adapting to changing energy demands and integrating renewable energy sources.

Cybersecurity Challenges in Smart Grids and Practical Implementation/Deployment

The increasing digitalization and interconnection of smart grids introduce significant cybersecurity challenges. The grid's critical infrastructure nature makes it a prime target for cyberattacks, which can disrupt power supply, damage equipment, and compromise sensitive data. Vulnerabilities in communication protocols, control systems, and data management platforms can be exploited by malicious actors. Denial-of-service attacks can overload grid infrastructure, while malware infections can compromise control systems. Data breaches can expose sensitive consumer information and operational data. To address these challenges, robust cybersecurity measures are essential. Implementing strong authentication and access control mechanisms, encrypting communication channels, and deploying intrusion detection and prevention systems are crucial. Secure coding practices and regular security audits are also necessary to identify and mitigate vulnerabilities. Practical implementation involves deploying secure communication protocols like IEC 62351, implementing Public Key Infrastructure (PKI) for secure device authentication, and using Security Information and Event Management (SIEM) systems for real-time threat detection. Deploying firewalls and network segmentation can limit the impact of cyberattacks. Implementing a layered security approach, with defense-in-depth strategies, is vital. Regular security training for personnel and continuous monitoring of grid infrastructure are also essential for maintaining a secure and resilient smart grid.

AUTONOMOUS VEHICLES AND INTELLIGENT TRANSPORTATION SYSTEMS

Sensor Fusion and Perception, Decision-Making/Control Algorithms

Autonomous vehicles (AVs) and intelligent transportation systems (ITS) rely on advanced sensor fusion and perception to understand their surroundings. Sensor fusion combines data from multiple sensors, such as lidar, radar, cameras, and ultrasonic sensors, to create a comprehensive and accurate representation of the environment. Lidar provides high-resolution 3D point clouds, radar detects objects at long distances, cameras provide visual information, and ultrasonic sensors detect objects at close range. Perception algorithms process this sensor data to detect and track objects, recognize traffic signs and lane markings, and estimate the vehicle's position and orientation. Decision-making and control algorithms use this perception data to plan and execute safe and efficient driving maneuvers. Path planning algorithms determine the optimal trajectory for the vehicle, taking into account traffic conditions, road geometry, and vehicle dynamics. Control algorithms regulate the vehicle's speed, steering, and braking to follow the planned trajectory. Machine learning techniques, such as deep learning, are increasingly used for perception and decision-making, enabling AVs to learn from experience and adapt to complex driving scenarios.

Communication/Connectivity and Security Considerations for Autonomous Vehicles

Communication and connectivity are essential for AVs and ITS. Vehicle-to-everything (V2X) communication enables vehicles to exchange information with other vehicles (V2V), infrastructure (V2I), pedestrians (V2P), and the network (V2N). V2X communication enhances situational awareness, improves traffic flow, and enables cooperative driving maneuvers. Cellular networks and dedicated short-range communications (DSRC) provide the communication infrastructure for V2X. Cloud connectivity enables AVs to access real-time traffic information, map data, and software updates. Security considerations are paramount for AVs, as cyberattacks can have catastrophic consequences. Vulnerabilities in communication channels, sensor systems, and control algorithms can be exploited by malicious actors. Implementing secure communication protocols, encrypting data, and deploying intrusion detection and prevention systems are crucial. Secure coding practices and regular security audits are also necessary to identify and mitigate vulnerabilities. Over-the-air (OTA) software updates must be securely delivered and installed to prevent tampering. Hardware security modules (HSMs) can be used to protect cryptographic keys and sensitive data. Implementing a layered security approach, with defense-in-depth strategies, is vital. Regular security testing and penetration testing are also essential for ensuring the security of AVs.

INDUSTRY 4.0 AND SMART MANUFACTURING (2 PAGES)

Industrial IoT (IIoT) and Digital Twins, Robotics/Automation in Manufacturing

Industry 4.0 represents a paradigm shift in manufacturing, driven by the integration of digital technologies. The Industrial Internet of Things (IIoT) connects machines, sensors, and devices on the factory floor, enabling real-time data collection and analysis. Digital twins are virtual replicas of physical assets, processes, or systems, allowing for simulation, optimization, and predictive maintenance. Robotics and automation play a crucial role in smart manufacturing. Collaborative robots (cobots) work alongside human workers, performing repetitive or dangerous tasks. Automated guided vehicles (AGVs) transport materials and products within the factory. Advanced manufacturing systems, such as additive manufacturing (3D printing), enable the production of customized and complex parts. IIoT platforms collect data from sensors and machines, providing insights into production processes, equipment performance, and product quality. Digital twins enable manufacturers to simulate and optimize production processes, identify bottlenecks, and predict equipment failures. Robotics and automation enhance productivity, reduce costs, and improve product quality.

Predictive Maintenance/Quality Control and Cybersecurity in Industrial Environments

Predictive maintenance uses data analytics and machine learning to predict equipment failures before they occur, minimizing downtime and maintenance costs. Sensors monitor equipment parameters, such as vibration, temperature, and pressure, and data analytics algorithms identify patterns that indicate potential failures. Quality control systems use machine vision and other sensing technologies to inspect products and identify defects. Real-time data analysis enables manufacturers to identify and correct quality issues early in the production process. Cybersecurity is a critical concern in industrial environments, as cyberattacks can disrupt production, damage equipment, and compromise sensitive data. Vulnerabilities in IIoT devices, control systems, and communication networks can be exploited by malicious actors. Implementing strong authentication and access control mechanisms, encrypting communication channels, and deploying intrusion detection and prevention systems are crucial. Secure coding practices and regular security audits are also necessary to identify and mitigate vulnerabilities. Network segmentation and firewalls can limit the impact of cyberattacks. Implementing a layered security approach, with defense-in-depth strategies, is vital. Regular security training for personnel and continuous monitoring of industrial control systems are also essential for maintaining a secure and resilient industrial environment.

FUTURE TRENDS AND CHALLENGES

1. ARTIFICIAL INTELLIGENCE AND MACHINE LEARNING ADVANCEMENTS

The Expanding Frontier of AI and ML

Artificial Intelligence (AI) and Machine Learning (ML) are rapidly transforming industries and daily life. The advancements in these fields are driven by the confluence of increased computational power, vast datasets, and innovative algorithms. Deep learning, a subset of ML, has particularly revolutionized areas like computer vision, natural language processing, and robotics. Convolutional Neural Networks (CNNs) have achieved remarkable accuracy in image recognition and object detection, enabling applications like autonomous driving and medical imaging. Recurrent Neural Networks (RNNs) and Transformers have significantly improved natural language processing, leading to breakthroughs in machine translation, chatbots, and sentiment analysis. Reinforcement learning, another powerful technique, allows agents to learn optimal policies through trial and error, enabling applications like game playing, robotics control, and resource management. Generative Adversarial Networks (GANs) have pushed the boundaries of creative AI, generating realistic images, videos, and music. The democratization of AI tools and platforms has enabled developers and researchers to rapidly prototype and deploy AI-powered applications. Cloud-based AI services provide access to pre-trained models and scalable infrastructure, lowering the barrier to entry for AI development.

The Practical Applications and Future Directions of AI/ML

The practical applications of AI and ML are vast and continue to expand. In healthcare, AI is used for disease diagnosis, drug discovery, and personalized medicine. In finance, AI is used for fraud detection, risk management, and algorithmic trading. In manufacturing, AI is used for predictive maintenance, quality control, and process optimization. In transportation, AI is used for autonomous vehicles, traffic management, and logistics optimization. The future of AI and ML holds immense potential. Explainable AI (XAI) is gaining traction, aiming to make AI models more transparent and interpretable, addressing concerns about bias and accountability. Federated learning, a technique that enables training models on decentralized data, is addressing privacy concerns and enabling collaborative AI development. AI at the edge is enabling real-time processing and decision-making on devices, reducing latency and bandwidth requirements. Neuro-symbolic AI, which combines neural networks with symbolic reasoning, is aiming to create more robust and adaptable AI systems. AI is also being used to address societal challenges, such as climate change, poverty, and inequality. The continued development of AI and ML will require ethical considerations, responsible innovation, and collaboration between researchers, policymakers, and industry leaders.

2. EDGE COMPUTING AND FOG COMPUTING (2 PAGES)

The Rise of Distributed Computing

Edge computing and fog computing are emerging paradigms that bring computation and data storage closer to the data source, addressing the limitations of traditional cloud computing. Edge computing involves processing data on devices or servers located at the network's edge, while fog computing involves processing data on intermediate devices or servers between the edge and the cloud. These paradigms are driven by the increasing volume of data generated by IoT devices, the need for real-time processing, and the limitations of bandwidth and latency associated with cloud computing. Edge computing enables devices to make local decisions and take immediate actions, reducing latency and improving responsiveness. Fog computing provides a distributed layer of computing resources that can filter, aggregate, and process data before sending it to the cloud. These paradigms enable applications like real-time analytics, autonomous driving, and industrial automation. Edge computing and fog computing are complementary, with edge computing focusing on local processing and fog computing focusing on distributed processing. The deployment of edge and fog computing requires careful consideration of security, privacy, and resource management.

Practical Applications and Challenges of Edge/Fog Computing

The practical applications of edge computing and fog computing are diverse and growing. In industrial automation, edge computing enables real-time control of machinery and robots, improving efficiency and reducing downtime. In smart cities, edge computing enables real-time traffic management, environmental monitoring, and public safety applications. In healthcare, edge computing enables remote patient monitoring, telemedicine, and personalized medicine. In retail, edge computing enables personalized shopping experiences, inventory management, and security monitoring. In autonomous driving, edge computing enables real-time decision-making and object detection. The challenges of edge computing and fog computing include security, privacy, and resource management. Security concerns include data breaches, device tampering, and denial-of-service attacks. Privacy concerns include data collection and sharing. Resource management concerns include efficient allocation of computing and storage resources. The development of standardized platforms and protocols is crucial for enabling interoperability and scalability. The integration of AI and ML at the edge is enabling intelligent edge devices that can learn and adapt to their environment. The deployment of edge computing and fog computing requires careful planning and implementation, considering the specific requirements of the application and the environment.

3. 5G AND NEXT-GENERATION COMMUNICATION
Revolutionizing Connectivity

5G and next-generation communication technologies are poised to revolutionize connectivity, enabling a wide range of new applications and services. 5G offers significantly higher data speeds, lower latency, and increased network capacity compared to previous generations. These advancements enable applications like augmented reality (AR), virtual reality (VR), and ultra-reliable low-latency communication (URLLC). 5G's ability to support a massive number of connected devices enables the deployment of large-scale IoT networks. Network slicing, a feature of 5G, allows for the creation of virtual networks tailored to specific applications, such as autonomous driving, industrial automation, and healthcare. 5G's ability to support mobile edge computing (MEC) enables real-time processing and decision-making at the network's edge. The deployment of 5G requires significant infrastructure investments, including the installation of small cells and the upgrade of core network equipment. The development of 6G and other next-generation communication technologies is already underway, aiming to further enhance connectivity and enable new applications.

The Impact and Future of Next-Gen Communication

The impact of 5G and next-generation communication technologies will be profound, transforming industries and daily life. In healthcare, 5G enables remote surgery, telemedicine, and personalized medicine. In transportation, 5G enables autonomous vehicles, traffic management, and logistics optimization. In manufacturing, 5G enables industrial automation, predictive maintenance, and quality control. In entertainment, 5G enables immersive AR/VR experiences, cloud gaming, and live streaming. The future of next-generation communication technologies holds immense potential. The integration of AI and ML with 5G will enable intelligent networks that can adapt to changing conditions and optimize performance. The development of new communication protocols and standards will enable the deployment of new applications and services. The convergence of communication, computing, and sensing technologies will enable the creation of new cyber-physical systems. The deployment of next-generation communication technologies requires careful consideration of security, privacy, and spectrum management. The collaboration between researchers, policymakers, and industry leaders is crucial for ensuring the successful deployment and adoption of these technologies.

ETHICAL CONSIDERATIONS AND SOCIETAL IMPACT (2 PAGES)

Navigating the Ethical Landscape

The rapid advancement of technology raises significant ethical considerations and societal impacts. AI and ML algorithms can perpetuate biases and discrimination, leading to unfair or unjust outcomes. The use of facial recognition technology raises concerns about privacy and surveillance. The deployment of autonomous weapons raises concerns about accountability and control. The increasing automation of jobs raises concerns about unemployment and social inequality. The use of data analytics raises concerns about data privacy and security. The development of new technologies requires careful consideration of their potential impacts on society. The development of ethical frameworks and guidelines is crucial for ensuring responsible innovation. The collaboration between researchers, policymakers, and industry leaders is essential for addressing ethical concerns. The education of the public about the ethical implications of technology is crucial for informed decision-making.

Shaping a Responsible Future

The societal impact of technology is profound and far-reaching. Technology can be used to address societal challenges, such as climate change, poverty, and inequality. Technology can also be used to create new opportunities for education, healthcare, and economic development. The development of inclusive and equitable technologies is crucial for ensuring that everyone benefits from technological advancements. The protection of human rights and dignity is essential in the development and deployment of new technologies. The promotion of digital literacy and access is crucial for ensuring that everyone can participate in the digital economy. The development of sustainable technologies is crucial for protecting the environment. The creation of a responsible and ethical technology ecosystem requires collaboration between researchers, policymakers, industry leaders, and civil society. The future of technology depends on our ability to navigate the ethical landscape and shape a responsible future.

THE INCREASING IMPORTANCE OF DIGITAL TWINS (2 PAGES)

Virtualizing the Physical World

Digital twins are virtual representations of physical assets, processes, or systems. They provide a dynamic and real-time reflection of their physical counterparts, enabling simulation, analysis, and optimization. Digital twins are created by collecting data from sensors, IoT devices, and other sources, and then using this data to build a virtual model. Digital twins are used in a wide range of industries, including manufacturing, healthcare, transportation, and infrastructure. In manufacturing, digital twins are used for predictive maintenance, process optimization, and quality control. In healthcare, digital twins are used for personalized medicine, drug discovery, and surgical planning. In transportation, digital twins are used for autonomous vehicle development, traffic management, and logistics optimization. In infrastructure, digital twins are used for building management, smart city planning, and energy grid optimization. Digital twins enable organizations to improve efficiency, reduce costs, and enhance decision-making.

SIX

CONCLUSION

The journey through this practical guide has illuminated the intricate landscape of Intelligent Cyber-Physical Systems (ICPS), revealing their transformative potential and the critical considerations necessary for their successful implementation. From the foundational principles of resilience and fault tolerance to the cutting-edge advancements in AI, 5G, and digital twins, we've explored the multifaceted dimensions of this rapidly evolving domain. As we stand at the cusp of a new era of automation and connectivity, the imperative to build secure, reliable, and ethical ICPS has never been more pressing.

We've underscored the importance of a holistic approach to ICPS development, one that seamlessly integrates hardware, software, and networking components. The significance of robust authentication and access control mechanisms, coupled with encryption and data protection strategies, cannot be overstated. These foundational security measures are the bedrock upon which trust and reliability are built. Intrusion detection and prevention systems, along with firewalls and secure communication protocols, form a formidable defense against the ever-evolving cyber threat landscape. We've also delved into the critical role of resilience and fault tolerance, emphasizing the need for redundancy, diversity, and effective fault detection and recovery mechanisms. Cyber-physical resilience, in particular, demands a proactive approach to mitigating the impact of attacks and failures, ensuring that systems can adapt and recover gracefully. The practical implementation of these principles has been a central theme, with case studies illustrating the real-world challenges and solutions in domains such as smart grids, autonomous vehicles, and Industry 4.0. We've explored the diverse array of development tools and platforms, from programming languages and frameworks to simulation and modeling tools, cloud platforms, and open-source libraries. These tools empower developers to build and deploy sophisticated ICPS, while adhering to best practices for security and resilience. The advancements in AI and ML, edge computing, 5G, and digital twins are driving the next wave of innovation in ICPS. These technologies are enabling the creation of intelligent systems that can learn, adapt, and interact with the physical world in unprecedented ways. However, with these advancements come significant ethical considerations and societal impacts. We must prioritize responsible innovation, ensuring that ICPS are developed and deployed in a manner that benefits society as a whole.

Looking ahead, the future of ICPS presents both immense opportunities and formidable challenges. The increasing complexity of these systems necessitates a continued focus on security, reliability, and scalability. The integration of AI and ML into ICPS will require careful consideration of bias, transparency, and accountability. The proliferation of IoT devices and the growing reliance on edge computing will demand robust security measures to protect against distributed attacks. The deployment of 5G and next-generation communication technologies will enable new applications and services, but also introduce new security vulnerabilities. The development of digital twins will revolutionize industries, but also raise concerns about data privacy and security. The ethical implications of ICPS, particularly in areas such as autonomous systems and AI-driven decision-making, will require ongoing dialogue and collaboration between researchers, policymakers, and industry leaders. The need for standardized protocols and frameworks will become increasingly critical as ICPS become more interconnected and interoperable. The convergence of cyber and physical domains will necessitate a multidisciplinary approach to security, encompassing both technical and operational aspects. The role of human-in-the-loop will continue to be vital, especially in critical applications where safety and reliability are paramount. The education and training of a skilled workforce will be essential for the successful development and deployment of ICPS. The importance of continuous monitoring, auditing, and maintenance of ICPS cannot be overstated. Regular security assessments and penetration testing are crucial for identifying and mitigating vulnerabilities. The use of threat intelligence and vulnerability management systems will enable organizations to proactively address security risks. The development of incident response plans and disaster recovery strategies will ensure that organizations can effectively respond to and recover from security incidents and system failures.

In conclusion, Intelligent Cyber-Physical Systems represent a powerful force for innovation and progress. However, their potential can only be fully realized if we prioritize security, reliability, and ethical considerations. The practical guide presented here serves as a roadmap for building a responsible and secure ICPS ecosystem. It is a call to action for developers, researchers, policymakers, and industry leaders to collaborate and address the challenges and opportunities that lie ahead. We must embrace a proactive and holistic approach to security, integrating security measures into every stage of the ICPS lifecycle. We must foster a culture of resilience, designing systems that can withstand and recover from failures. We must prioritize ethical considerations, ensuring that ICPS are developed and deployed in a manner that benefits society as a whole. We must invest in education and training, empowering a skilled workforce to build and maintain secure ICPS. We must foster collaboration and information sharing, creating a community that can collectively address the challenges of this evolving domain. By embracing these principles, we can harness the transformative power of ICPS to create a safer, more efficient, and more sustainable future. The journey towards a secure and intelligent future with Cyber-Physical Systems is ongoing, and it requires the collective effort of all stakeholders. Let us embrace the challenge and build a future where technology empowers us to create a better world for all.

www.ingramcontent.com/pod-product-compliance
Lightning Source LLC
Chambersburg PA
CBHW062219150726

47991CB00006B/2354